THE TWO COMMANDMENTS OF CHRIST

The Two Commandments of Christ

FRANCIS J. McGARRIGLE, S.J.

Agrégé, Gregorian University, Rome
Professor of Ethics, Seattle University

THE BRUCE PUBLISHING COMPANY • MILWAUKEE

IMPRIMI POTEST:

ALEXANDER F. McDONALD, S.J.
Praep. Prov. Oregon. S.J.

NIHIL OBSTAT:

JOHN A. SCHULIEN, S.T.D.
Censor librorum

IMPRIMATUR:

✠ WILLIAM E. COUSINS
Archbishop of Milwaukee
January 23, 1962

Library of Congress Catalog Card Number: 62–16839

© 1962 THE BRUCE PUBLISHING COMPANY
MADE IN THE UNITED STATES OF AMERICA

*To my beloved Mother, the Society of Jesus,
especially to those many self-sacrificing
Coadjutor Brothers, Ministers, and Administrators,
nameless perhaps on earth, but celebrities in heaven,
who have freed me from material cares,
affording me thousands of extra hours for writing
this their Book for whatever good it can do.*

FOREWORD

In birth, as a creature that will know and love, man enters into a natural solidarity of love between himself and God. Made social in nature, man enters also into a natural solidarity of love between himself and all mankind.

In his divine birth of Baptism, man enters into the solidarity of the mutual love of the Trinity and into the Mystical Body of Christ, the Church. This was expressed by early Christians as entrance into "the Union," into "the Love."

On these human and divine solidarities of love, inspired Christian masters have from the beginning composed theological symphonies which have majestically rolled down the halls of the ages. To them I join my oaten stop, with the fond wish that, in this world of man's opprobrious discord with God and man's inhuman discord with man, its thin and simple strain may attract some ear to the harmony of love for which alone man was made.

CONTENTS

I. LOVE THY NEIGHBOR

I. THE NATURE OF FRATERNAL CHARITY

1. *"The Milk of Human Kindness"*

As much as a baby needs milk, we need kindness. Hence it is called in more than one tongue "the milk of human kindness." Fraternal charity or love of others — which is wishing others well and doing them good because they are fellow children of God — is an absolute need for all men. It is necessary for both the giver of kindness and for the receiver. In fact, the giver needs to give his kindness more than others need to receive it, great as their need is.

We owe sincere gratitude to those we help for the opportunity they give us to exercise a function indispensable to our own welfare. We do not sufficiently realize that the obligation of perfecting others by kindness helps us fulfill our obligation to glorify God and grow in perfection ourselves.

God made man essentially and inescapably social. The relations we have to other persons reach so intimately into the inner recesses of our mind, our soul, our very being, that there cannot be a normal individual life, not even a contemplative religious life, which is not at the same time social. Because he has a mind and will, man is gregarious. It follows that man realizes God's purpose for him in two ways: first, in his personal morality; second, in his relations with his fellows, which give rise to social morality. Without love for others, individual life is a corpse; its soul is gone. Family life without love is an empty house; its tenant is gone. International life without love is the house of the insane; reason is gone.

The palace of fraternal love, in which live the princes and princesses of mankind, is a towering edifice of unsuspected complexity. To build it, we must do some mental digging to a bedrock of fundamental fact; and only on this can we proceed to raise a reasoned framework of interwelded principles on which the whole structure is upheld. Many persons, including, and especially, many intellectuals, attempt to build and live in an edifice of fraternal love which neither rests on reasonably solid motivation, nor is it supported throughout by connected girder principles. To a passing glance it may appear a fairly sound construction, but under a little rational probing or emotional pressure it cannot hang together and it collapses into disconnected and unsupported sentimental rubble, unfit to house the being of intelligence and emotion that is man. So let us first bare our bedrock foundation and on it raise our network of girder principles.

It is God's purpose that as social creatures we love others and be loved by them, His children whom He loves. "Wherever there is a human being, there kindness is in order."[1] When He placed us in the midst of others, God gave us the important commission through our social natures: Be My providence for them! Be My love for them! So the Greek poet said: "Man helping man is God helping man."

By raising our natural social life, through grace, to supernatural social life in the Mystical Body, God has correspondingly raised our social purpose to the supernatural order. In natural fraternal love, we are kind to another because he has a social human nature, which our common Creator intends us to endeavor to perfect; and thus we give God glory by our social perfection. But natural kindness, great as it may be, is not sufficient. Since man has a supernatural end, supernatural kindness is required, kindness given while in the state of grace. In supernatural fraternal love, we allow the Christ dwelling in us to be kind, through our kind thoughts, words, and actions, to the Christ dwelling in others, either through grace or through their representation of Him, according to His arrangement that whatever we do to the least of them we do to Him (Mt. 25:40).

Raguel embraced and kissed the young Tobias and wept over him (Tob. 7:1 ff.) because he saw in him close resemblance to his own brother, the elder Tobias, and not for any other reason, as he had never seen him before. So we are to love our neighbor because we see our Brother Christ in him. Our fellow man does not lose this

---

[1] Seneca, *Thestes*, 214.

title to our love merely because he may be disagreeable to us on account of his character, circumstances, or even his injuries to us. He is always the brother of Christ.

We are inclined to judge the worth of our love for our neighbor by the amount of good we do to him and, perhaps, by the amount of self-sacrifice in that love. But these are relatively minor factors in its worth. The one correct appraisal of the act of love of neighbor, as of every other act, is the extent to which it is supernatural.

Christian fraternal love is that of adopted children of God. To love others merely because they are fellow human beings is not enough. Through divinizing grace, we must love others as Christ loves us: "As the Father has loved me [His divine Son], I also have loved you" (Jn. 15:9), His divine children and My brethren. All supernatural glory to God, for which alone man exists, must be through, with, and in the Son dwelling in us. This glory to God requires grace and depends mostly on the amount of sanctifying grace accompanying the act of kindness. Of course, given equal sanctifying grace in us, the more difficult our act of charity is, the more we glorify God and the more grace we receive as merit.

2. *"As I Have Loved You"*

Human love is totally justified because in loving others we love God. Yet we do not love our neighbor because of God merely as a *fictio juris*. We do not love him as we love money which in itself is only a paper sign, which we don't love, of values which we do love. Our neighbor is not merely a sign of God but also the object of our love. Again, we do not love God in our neighbor as though God were far away from him. Naturally, his Creator, Preserver, and Co-operator is in him while supernaturally through grace God is the divinizing principle of his person and life. Our supernatural love of neighbor is immeasurably more noble and intense than any possible natural love. In grace we love him as Christ loves him. The act of love of our neighbor, as Christ intends it, is love "through Christ." Philanthropy without grace is not Christian love of neighbor, for all that is Christian must be done "in Christ," in sanctifying grace.

Still, because we are human, human motives do enter into our love for others, and such motives can even intensify our love of Christ. Christ in us can elevate these human motives and supernaturalize them. On the other hand, if charity toward someone is actually repugnant to us, the performing of an act of kindness for him is especially pleasing to God and meritorious.

Christ gave us a new commandment: "that you love one another: that as I have loved you, you also love one another" (Jn. 13:34). This means that we are to love others, not merely because they are valuable in our eyes, but because they are worth much to Christ and because in loving them we express our love for Christ. St. Thomas says: "No strictly true virtue is possible without charity,"[2] love of God. This love gives life and meaning to all other virtues, using them as means to express itself.

An act of love of neighbor is not essentially different from an act of love of God, of which it is merely a mode, an application, and a consequence. St. Thomas writes:

> . . . it is specifically the same visual act whereby we see the light and whereby we see color under the aspect of light . . . it is specifically the same act whereby we love God and whereby we love our neighbor.[3]

Love of God is the first principle in all correct loving. Because of it we are to love everything else. I love my neighbor principally because I love God; I do not love God principally because I love my neighbor. "Love of God," says St. John Chrysostom, "is united with love of man, as the soul is to the body. He who loves the Father, loves the child of the Father."[4] As the likeness we have to God is prior to, and the cause of, the likeness we have to our fellows, so the love we have for God must be prior to, and the cause of, the love we have for our fellows.

Christ asked Peter three times, "Dost thou love me more than these [other apostles] do?" (Jn. 21:15.) As a consequence of Peter's threefold humble affirmation of love of Him, Christ enjoined him

---

[2] *Summa Theologiae*, II–II, q. 23, a. 7.

[3] *Ibid.*, q. 25, a. 1.

[4] *Hom.* 32 in 1 Cor. *PG* 61, 272.

three times to love the members of His Mystical Body: "Feed My lambs; feed My sheep"; that is, if you love Me, you will devotedly cherish and love and care for My lambs and My sheep, My brethren.

For this reason, real love can't go wrong; "love and do as you will." It is hate, sometimes masquerading as love, which is harmful. "Love does no evil" (Rom. 13:10). There are two pillars to the porticoes of paradise, our Lord tells us: "love of God with our whole soul" and "love of our neighbor as ourselves." This also holds for paradise in this world, as far as it can be had.

Truth and beauty and happiness can come only into a world whose real purpose is preserved. We must see things as God sees them, perfectly, truly; and God sees our neighbor as possessing a value and importance, by and large, equal to our own. No man can be for himself alone, if God is for us all.

God gave us a strong instinct to seek our own good. Through our nature He imposes on us an inescapable love of ourselves. And it is with the same kind of love that He wants us freely to love our neighbor. Hence the homely adage: "Do unto others as you would have them do to you." Atheism has no basis for the divine and difficult doctrine that we are to love others as ourselves; it is only when we "love God with our whole soul" that we can love our neighbor "as ourselves."

But how are we to love others "as ourselves"? Perhaps some distinctions here would be of help. We cannot love our neighbor with the same instinctive *spontaneity* "as" we love ourselves. Our nature obliges us to wish well to ourselves; we cannot wish ourselves evil, unless we see it as in some way good for us.

If we understand love of our neighbor as love of *benevolence* — as wishing him well — we must wish ourselves well in preference to others, inasmuch as our one purpose in existence is to perfect our natures as God's glory. This is God's primary extrinsic purpose in creation, and must be the primary intrinsic purpose of our actions, if we live according to the truth. However, we can do good to our social natures only by doing good to others.

If we understand love of our neighbor as love of *complacency*, that is, delight in his natural perfection, which is his glory to God, then we can love him "as" ourselves, or even more than ourselves.

For he has a value and perfection of nature equal to or greater than our own, equally or more adequately reflecting God's perfection and glory, which is the measure of all worth and lovableness.

3. *"Whatever You Do to Them You Do to Me"*

Christ revealed the sublime essence of Christian love of neighbor. The Old Testament taught a love of neighbor based on the natural law: "Thou shalt love thy friend as thyself. I am the Lord" (Lev. 19:18). Since God is the Creator Lord, His human creatures must love one another as children of the same heavenly Father. Christ makes love of neighbor a new commandment by bidding us to love our neighbor as He loves us. How much is that, O Christ? By the facts of His life He answers:

> I lived My Life and died My death for you;
> I loved you gratuitously, with no advantage to Myself;
> I loved you all, especially "the little ones," the underprivileged;
> I loved you for the love of My Father;
> Above all, I loved you as the Son of the Father and as your
>   Brother adopting you in grace.
>   This is what it means to love others as I have loved you.

St. Paul consequently says that Christians are no longer in the servitude of the Old Law, while he reminds them that their freedom as children of God in the New Law requires them to serve one another. This is "to walk in the Holy Spirit."

> For you, brethren, have been called to liberty . . . by charity serve one another (Gal. 5:13). . . . If we live by the [Holy] Spirit, by the [Holy] Spirit let us also walk [act]. Let us not become desirous of vainglory, provoking one another, envying one another (*ibid.*, 25–26) .

The Apostle himself practices this self-sacrificing love of others for pure love of Christ:

> I will most gladly spend [all I have] and be spent myself for your souls, even though, loving you more, I be loved less (2 Cor. 12:15).

St. John, the apostle of divine love, in his Gospel and letters, especially seeks to instill and develop love of God which must be the reason and basis for rational love of one another. While Paul more frequently proposes the Mystical Body as the source of our duty to love God and neighbor, St. John more frequently bases this duty on the very nature of God who is Love, and the clear command of Christ: "Love as I have loved you."

> Beloved, let us love one another, for love is from God. And everyone who loves is born of God, and knows God. He who does not love does not know God; for God is love. . . . Beloved, if God has so loved us, we also ought to love one another. No one has ever seen God. If we love one another, God abides in us and his love is perfected in us. In this we know that we abide in him, and he in us, because he has given us of his Spirit (1 Jn. 4:7–13).

From the wonderful truth of Christ, the one Life by which all souls live who live a supernatural life, there follows the marvelous truth, unknown and nonexistent before the Son of God became man, of the incomparable solidarity of Christian fraternal love, such as exists between parts of the same body which live the same life. In the words of St. Paul:

> I, therefore, the prisoner in the Lord, exhort you to walk in a manner worthy of the calling with which you were called, with all humility and meekness, with patience, bearing with one another in love, careful to preserve the unity of the Spirit in the bond of peace: one body and one Spirit, even as you were called in one hope of your calling; one Lord, one faith, one baptism; one God and Father of all, who is above all, and throughout all, and in us all (Eph. 4:1–6).

In these words Paul echoes the basic teaching of his divine Master at the Last Supper that we should love one another as divine brethren. We should do so because we share in the life of Christ, and thus we should all be one in Him, as He is in the Father and the Father is in Him.

The reason which nature gives for mutual love among children of the same parents is the bond of family, the tie of common parents who have given the children their life and nourishment and protection and love. He who does not love his sisters and brothers is

considered abnormal. Now, the fundamental fact that we are creatures of God gives all men a closer brotherhood than that of family.
Our earthly parents are instruments used by God to commence
new life, while God is the Parent who not only gives the beginning
of life to all, but also, instant by instant, pours being, life, and action
into us, as He pours it into everything else that has influence on us.

This common paternity of God constitutes the absolute brotherhood of man. Man could not be man unless he were a brother.
But, with the supernatural communication of the divine life in
grace, and with the consequent adoption of man as the brother
and sister of Christ and as the supernatural child of the Father,
Christ has raised natural fraternal love to a Christian beauty and
sublimity. This love is in proportion to the beauty and sublimity
of the participated divine life which renders man "another Christ"
and another beloved child in whom the Father is well pleased.
Christ pours into us divine being, divine life, and divine action,
finite sharings in His own being, life, and action. Thus my fellow
in grace can claim my love, not only as a creature of the same
Creator, but also as the adopted divine child of the same divine
Father. He has an inviolable, irrefragable claim on my love when
he says: "It is now no longer I that live, but Christ lives in me"
(Gal. 2:20). In the light of grace, what a glow, what a warmth is in
those words of Christ: "Amen I say to you, as long as you did it
for one of these, the least of my brethren, you did it for me" (Mt.
25:40). "Do not draw your sword to strike Christ, O Christian!" is
St. Augustine's warning.[5] When we look on our neighbor as a
fellow child of God, we see our obligation to love him equally as
ourselves. When we look on him as Christ's representative, and still
more when we contemplate him as Christ indwelling in him, we
see that, as St. Paul instructs, we are to esteem all from our hearts as
our betters (Phil. 2:3).

This is the divinization of charity, according to St. Augustine:
"and so, there shall be one Christ loving Himself." No longer sight-
less, think of Christ in each, love Christ in each. Our neighbor,
affording us opportunity of realizing our love of God, is a signpost
guiding our journey to God. "We cannot see God, who is invisible,"

---

[5] *In Joan.* 5, n. 12; *PL* 35, 1420.

says St. Gregory the Great in one of his Homilies, "but we can find a way to Him through His servants, in whom He is reflected."

Christ has not only identified Himself with my neighbor as the object of my love; He has also supernaturally identified Himself with me loving them. He has identified His divine love with my Christian love. It is totally "in Christ." "As I have loved you, you also love one another" (Jn. 13:34). Indwelling in you — Christ says to us — I make use of your love to express My love for them, both in your soul and in your exterior acts. Allow Me to express Myself in you in the fullness of your love associated with My love.

Christ is not only the model of the love I must bear my neighbor; He is also the source of that love, as far as I allow Him to be. Actively engaged in the apostolate of charity, I must always seek the fructifying love of Christ in my love of man. Without Him my works are sterile.

As Christ's real life is His interior life, it is in my interior life, above all, that I must give His love of my neighbor full and untrammeled scope. St. Augustine says:

> If charity does not dwell there then neither does God. One would like, perhaps, to see God seated in heaven: if he has charity, God dwells in him just as truly as He dwells in heaven.[6]

Do you wish to know how to love others? Ask Jesus: How do You, dwelling in me, wish to love Your brothers? So intimately has Christ enveloped us and all humanity in Himself that we are tempted timidly to recoil from the consequences of our union with Him. Yet we form one body with Him — He the head, we the members — and thus, for instance, we are to love sinners, as Christ loved them, in living and dying for them.

Many companies have established credit for travelers through a credit card. With it they receive food, lodging, and other necessities, for which they pay in one payment from their bank deposit at home. God, as our Creator, Redeemer, and Sanctifier, has furnished every traveler on life's journey with a credit card. It represents Christ's credit for that most important necessity which no company can supply, credit for love from every man, and especially from every

---

[6] *In Psalm 149,* n. 4; *PL* 37, 1951.

Christian. And this credit, as our Lord taught St. Catherine of
Siena, is totally gratuitous. He has paid for all of it.

> All the love which you have for Me you owe to Me; so that it is
> not gratis that you love Me, while I love you gratis, and not
> because I owe you My love. Therefore, you cannot repay Me in
> person for the love which I require of you. So, I have placed you
> in the midst of your fellows, in order that you may do for them
> that which you cannot do for Me; that is, in order that you may
> love your neighbor gratis, without expecting any return from him.
> What you do to him, I count as done to Me.[7]

Our circumstances are the sacrament of God's will for us. Our
fellow human beings are the sacrament of His love. In both instances
our faith will find its test in our recognition of Him in them.
Children, the little brothers and sisters of our Lord, strew roses along
the way of their divine Brother in His Corpus Christi procession.
His declaration: "Whatever you do to them you do to Me," has made
us His flower children, to strew roses before Him, walking on earth
among our brethren.

4. The Social Christ

Materialistic sociologists cannot see that the nation's crime, dishon-
esty, racial and religious hate, injustice, family disruption, business
ruthlessness, and political cynicism are only surface manifestations,
the results, not the cause, of our vicious and unhappy society. One
does not need to be a Master in Social Science in order not to have
the trees cut off his view of the forest. There is little mystery as to
how society is to be saved. Reason without the support of revelation
is sufficient to point out the cure, although Christian-motivated self-
denial is needed to carry it out. What society needs is love of every
human being as a child of a common Creator-Father, God, and,
rising from this basic love, mutual tenderness and sympathy, generosity of the "haves," both individuals and nations, toward the
"have-nots." In a word, *Caritas,* love, would make the world a

[7] *Dialogue of St. Catherine of Siena,* trans. by A. Thorwald, p. 155.

paradise. Man is made for love, and it is strange that many are so long in making this discovery, while still others never discover this essential and universal factor of our social nature. Every human being is a loud cry, although his voice be mute, shouting for help — the help of love.

Not by any means on bread alone does man live. Living on bread alone, man will die psychologically. Nature, at times, asserts its need of love dispensed to others in emergency or catastrophe; and it is beautiful to contemplate the deep-red rose of love blossoming in the ruins of suffering.

The spirit of kindness generates peace. A nation is its individuals; and how can there be national or international peace, when there is so much unnecessary friction in our individual daily lives because we neglect to lubricate them with love? To how many, in our daily contacts, do we positively express kindness? All should feel, as the result of our contact with them, that we have kindly sentiments toward them; all should leave us revived and strengthened by our kindness. How does our voice sound? How do we appear, especially to those on whom we do not depend, but who depend on us? Are we fraternal and warm? In our family, are we invariably patient, tender, and understanding? Above all, when out of sorts or frustrated in our purposes, do we resist the tendency to "take it out on others"? Do we make this contribution of our self-restraint to the happiness of others, as an act of love of our Father, God? We can have the "abundant life" only by giving others the "abundant life" of kindness.

To the protest of the pseudo-realists that constant kindliness is an invitation to others to walk over you, ask them, who gets most out of life, not to speak of eternity: the person whose constant kindness is at times abused to his disadvantage, or the person who is not kindly lest he be abused? We cannot be saved, as individuals or as society, except as brothers. So the Creator made us. Our nature demands the practice and the regular reception of fraternal kindness.

Our Redeemer stressed that, after love of God, the love of our fellow is the most important realization of our redemption, both individual and social. Hence, as one would expect, kindness is eminently practical. When mankind has understood that both in theory and in practice there is no salvation outside of kindness, humanity will find itself back again where it belongs, in an earthly paradise, awaiting its transit to the heavenly paradise.

We have multitudes of teachers, with all kinds of degrees, who tell us how to make money, build bridges, construct polyradical molecules, live healthily, dress attractively, conduct a perfect cuisine and home, get the greatest athletic response from the body's muscles. But where are those competent to teach the principles and practice of indispensable brotherly love? Immeasurably more important than the above instructions for the family, for the nation, and for the world, is the propaganda of love of others — wishing well to all, and doing good to them as occasion offers.

Many are the social reforms to be made, at the levels of the family, of business, of the nation, and of the world's family of nations. But peace through treaty, through trade, through science, through a higher level of material living — and most of all through armament — is foolishly sought while the sole universal remedy, love, remains unused. Even Soviet hate is madly thought to be the road to cosmic happiness; and materialistic determinism attempts, with science and industrial production, to cure mankind's spiritual ills, which only spiritual love can cure. Why are individuals unhappy? Because they do not love individually. Why are there industrial conflicts? Because workers and employers have so little love for each other. Why are nations in conflict? Because of the lack of love between them.

5. *Love of Others Is Really Love of Self*

This rather startling statement is the norm and guide for altruism, to the extent that it is true egoism. The word *egoism* is commonly used in relation to hatred of one's ego. Here we use this term to signify real love of one's ego. Our statement of this truth, of which many are not clearly aware, is manifest from the following reasoning.

The purpose of God in creating man, and consequently the purpose of man's existence, is that he voluntarily be God's extrinsic glory. This glory is not something outside of man which he, as it were, gives to God. The extrinsic glory of God in all creatures is their perfection of nature and action, by which they are a finite imitation and reflection of God's infinite nature and activity, to the degree that he intends in creating each individual being.

Nonhuman beings reflect perfectly the glory that God intends in them; but theirs is a glory forced by the inviolable laws imposed on them. Man gives glory to God freely, inasmuch as his actions are voluntary, freely chosen to perfect his nature. There is no other way in which man can be the freely chosen glory of God but by what his action is and does to himself. It follows then that man's altruistic action has its value for him only in its egoism, or the perfecting of himself as his freely chosen glory of God.

In this way all love of others is self-love and all God's glory through us is also our own glory. The welfare of a man's society must always be understood by him only as an intermediate end and as means to his own perfection and welfare, by which, as the image of God, he can give Him glory. Thus man directs all things "through himself and with himself and in himself" to the glory of God. For this reason, generally, the better we live for others according to our circumstances, the more we live for ourselves and for God. For this reason, also, I may never do good to my society or to its members by acting contrary to the good of my own nature, which is God's glory. Thus, if I am an incurable invalid consuming all the money that my wife earns so that she and my children must live in a vicious and wretched slum, nevertheless I may not do them the service of committing suicide. I would indeed be doing them great good in making a decent life possible for them, but I would be acting against the good of my own nature and thereby against God's glory.

Even true love of God is also love of self. "Suppose," says Aquinas, "that God were not man's good; then man would have no reason for loving Him."[8] Even love of complacence, the mere desire that a thing be what it is, is a satisfaction of our inborn tendency to love the good merely because of what it is. "Art for art's sake" is always art for my sake. Man is to be freely "for himself," in imitation of God who is necessarily for Himself. The only way that man can be truly for himself is to be for God and to be for others, but never

---

[8] *Summa,* I, 60, 5, 2.

in such a way that in being for others he is not for himself, and consequently not for God. In this sense, as Shakespeare has the Dauphin say, "Self-love, my liege, is not so vile a sin as self-forgetting."[9]

Of course, I may at times value the result of my altruistic action as objectively greater than the glory of God achieved in my action. But I must always will my action, as such, that is, formally, because of its own glory to God. I also am to will my action's *result* because by so doing I perfect my nature and glorify God; but I must not will nor value glory to God from others by means of altruistic action which is against my nature. I may not act contrary to lawful authority no matter how much glory to God and good of souls is the result of my action. A morally evil means is not justified by its good end.

We personally glorify God, not by anything outside ourselves, but only by reflecting His perfection in ourselves. The perfection of others is *their* reflection and glory of God. We do not estimate the value of glory given to God by the *results* of our actions but by their intrinsic perfection; not because of what others are and do because of us, but because of what we are and do because of them. Thus, if I fulfill my social duties toward a person, say, a child or pupil, who subsequently does, or does not, live a life of glory to God, the glory I give to God is equal in both cases.

In brief, the norm and obligation of right ethical action in general is that the action perfect our nature as God's glory. From this it follows that the norm and obligation of social ethics, namely, in our relations with others, must be the perfecting of our natures as God's glory, and all our perfecting of others' lives is moral only to the extent that it is the perfecting of ourselves.

We must invest in the development of other lives in order to develop our own lives as God's glory. Even if the good will and efforts we invest in the welfare of others fail to have effect, we still receive the profit of our own betterment, of contributing to God's glory, and of attaining our greater beatitude in heaven. Only by spending my life for others can I save it for myself, above all, as a member of the Mystical Body. "He who shall lose his life shall find

---

[9] *Henry V*, 2, 4, 74.

it." The Creator has so fashioned human nature that if we do not live for others we do not live for ourselves. Yet moral altruism must be egoism.

This is the answer to the historian's query: Is history to be contemplated in its significance for society or in its meaning for individual men? History is, first of all, for the one unique God and for His eternal glory. This glory is achieved by God's communication of His goodness and perfection of life to each man in proportion as each man lives in accord with his nature, which is both social and personal. This is the answer to the Communist, whose basic belief is that all individual men exist wholly for the state, and not the state for the individual, and moreover, that they exist for that kind of Communist state which the Politburo happens to desire.

This understanding of altruism as enlightened egoism, and ultimately as theism, is the answer to those many educationalists who profess as the purpose of education the total "gearing of individuals to society," whatever it may be, or whatever they think it ought to be. How well Shakespeare expresses, as usual, the exact norm of human living which those administrators could adopt with much profit to the students:

> . . . To thine own self be true!
> And it must follow, as the night the day,
> Thou canst not then be false to any man.[10]

It is in order to ask here: What is the norm by which I know when and how self-sacrifice is moral? It is a problem that leaves secularist thinkers nonplused. While revelation teaches us the supernaturalizing of our actions and of their glory to God by grace, we settle this problem also by reasoning ethics.

Leaving out of the picture God and the next life, the secularist can offer no adequate motive for giving up our earthly good in favor of others, if we do not obtain thereby a greater earthly good, such as a deep satisfaction in the self-sacrifice. God's glory and beatitude are two cogent reasons for any sacrifice of earthly good. The good man loses nothing when he saves himself. Thus one brother reasonably sacrifices the great intellectual and spiritual good of a

---

[10] *Hamlet*, 1, 3, 70.

Catholic college education in favor of another when only one of them can obtain it. Here that which must be considered a great harm to our human nature, if we have only a materialist view of this life, appears as a great good when we know that God whom we thus please will more than recompense us. So we return to our original principle of self-aggrandizement as the justification of all moral self-sacrifice.

Fundamentally, then, the norm and obligation of doing good and avoiding evil to others must be absolute, rooted in a transcendent and infinite value. This can be only God's glory, in opposition to which one may not choose any other good. God's will as the good of our human nature is the only sufficient and rational motive for the occasional obligation to sacrifice one's own earthly good for the welfare of others, including at times our own very lives, for example, in defense of our country. On the other hand, as we must never do a good for others, so we must never sacrifice a good of our own for others when in either case we act against the natural law of perfecting our own nature in all action.

6. Ad Majorem Mei Gloriam

Just as we must will good to ourselves when we will good to others, so we cannot will harm to others without willing harm to ourselves. In fact, we are responsible for both good and evil willed to others precisely because it is good for or harmful to ourselves and to God's glory in us. When I poison my brother's spring, I must perish of thirst.

Spinoza, Wundt, Kant, and many others contend that an act is moral only when it is for the good of others, and that the actions we perform for our own good have no moral character, either good or bad. This shallow assertion of exclusively social ethics is offered as an immediately evident axiom; no proof is advanced in its defense. However, it is obvious that we cannot be morally perfected by the effect of our choices on others; and if, as they say, we cannot be perfected morally by the effect of our choices on ourselves, then no one can be moral. We must remember that society is not our end, but a means to it. Hence, "social service," by itself, cannot constitute the purpose of man, much less a religion.

This is one of the simplifications of the ethics of extreme evolutionists who hold that moral actions are solely social, in their origin, in their meaning, and in their purpose. Here, as usual, error gives itself the lie. This counter-evolutionary, out and out altruism is not what one would expect from the ground principle of evolution: "the survival of the fittest in the struggle for existence," "nature red in tooth and claw." Upstart, shaggy materialistic evolution borrows the finery of the natural law, but, like an upstart, carries it into impossible exaggeration which makes current evolutionary faith appear even worse than if it had remained in its natural and aboriginal crudity.

"Total disinterestedness," which many atheistic moralists cavalierly propose, is psychologically impossible; for we tend by nature to help others perfect themselves, as we tend to knowledge by nature. When we perfect others we perfect ourselves by satisfying an altruistic instinct just as we perfect ourselves when we satisfy our instinct for knowledge. We cannot do anything without seeking our good, real or apparent. The driving force of human activity is the desire to quench our thirst for good, and often the only way to accomplish this is to assist others in obtaining the good they need. For instance, in the satisfaction of her maternal instinct, the mother obtains her good by giving good to her children. So, in fulfilling social relationships, we receive a good, or satisfaction, of our social instinct.

Hence, for several reasons we must drastically modify Kant's "categorical imperative" that we treat all human beings always as an end, never as a means. True, we may not make our own or another's human nature merely the means to obtain earthly possessions. But we must use everything and everybody as means to our own human perfection, which is our sole means to attain the glory of God. In making others the supreme end of man, Kant unwittingly fathered the brood of modern sociomoralists.

In a sense not meant by Socrates, "I should bear injustice rather than do it." When I am unjust I injure my human nature in injuring others. When I reasonably bear injustice rather than do it, I benefit myself and make myself a greater glory of God as a more perfect human being; otherwise I should not bear injustice; and Socrates actually had no reason for his otherwise reasonable dictum.

Since we can give God no glory except by perfecting ourselves, we can well assert that there is no true altruism, which perfects our social nature, without true egoism. Strange how error skirts the truth! For we fittingly use evolutionist Spencer's social conclusion, which follows from his evolutionary premise of "survival of the fittest," namely, beneficence is justified only when "it is blessing to him that gives as well as blessing to him that receives."[11] All love is wasteful squandering which does not principally enrich self.

Man's nature is such that he must love himself in all his loving of other beings. Since we must fulfill God's purpose for us by giving ourselves to others, other human beings are indispensable means for glorifying God. Man cannot realize his God-intended perfection of self except by giving himself to something greater than himself: to God. And the neighbor, as God's representative, is his chief means to achieve this. Hence, the profound paradoxical truth of Christ's philosophy, which few understand well and fewer practice well, that by losing his life for his neighbor man loses his life for God, and thus finds it marvelously enhanced for himself.

Only God and immortality make us the center and hub of the world in all our actions, in which we, at once, give God and ourselves eternal glory. Only God and immortality make sense in the Socratic assertion that it is better to accept than to inflict injustice. Thus, ethics founded on true egoism makes social relations perfect, while an exclusively social ethics makes social relations a conflicting program. This, too, is the answer to Pascal's protest: "Self . . . is unjust because it makes self the center of all." Self is most fittingly the center of all creatures, inasmuch as the proper center of self is God's glory. We are an egocentric world because we are a theo-centric world. If we turn all our use of creatures to God's glory, we turn them all to our glory; and the purpose *ad majorem Dei*

---

[11] *Principles of Ethics,* part V, sec. 1.

gloriam (to the greater glory of God), becomes also *ad majorem mei gloriam* (to the greater glory of me).

St. Augustine observes:

Nothing seems to be said about our love of ourselves; yet when it is said: "Thou shalt love thy neighbor as thyself," it at once becomes evident that our love for ourselves has not been overlooked [by Christ].[12]

In founding a religion of love, Christ made the assumption, as epigrammatic as it is fundamental, that man loves himself, in order to demand of man supreme love of God and love of his neighbor as himself. Our love leads from weakness; we need to love others in order to enrich ourselves by enriching them. God's love of us leads from strength, in order to give goodness as a reflection of His own goodness.

7. *No Man Is Wholly for the Common Good*

Man is a social part of the universe and of human society, only analogically — not in the same sense as an arm is a part of the body, or as an object in a landscape painting is a part of the whole picture, or as a star, or an animal, or a tree, is a part of the whole universe. Such creatures are wholly subservient to the totality of which they are parts. Man is a person with inalienable rights, obligations, and destiny which are not totally subservient to any created whole, but only to God. All other things, as St. Ignatius says in his *Spiritual Exercises,* are means to carry out his destiny — not because man is to consider himself worth more than all else, but because God wills him to perfect himself as His glory, and God's glory is of infinitely more worth than all else. In this sense, every human being must use every other human being for his own perfection.

True, man must largely co-operate toward the common good, thus imitating his Creator, in order to obtain his own good and the con-

---

[12] *On Christian Doctrine* I, 26.

sequent glory of God. But man must look on the common good of
a group always and without exception as a means to his own good,
despite many "altruists" who contend that "the greatest good of
the greatest number" decides the right and wrong of all action for
all individuals.

Aristotle's ethics, making each person's good wholly subordinate
to the good of the State is an unjustified concept. Each person is
a cosmos in himself, and his interests are not wholly subject to the
interests of the State nor to the common good of any society. This
doctrine is anathema to all forms of totalitarianism, especially to
that of Communism.

Homo homini sacra res: to man, man is sacred; that is, his nature's
own good is *consecrated* to God's glory as to his ultimate and absolute end. The common good may not profane this consecrated being
by subjecting man wholly to itself. All man's subjection to the common good must be in his own best interest. To deny the sacredness
of man is, in effect, to deny the source of that sacredness, God Himself. Great and noble as was Plato's idea of man, and far surpassing
that of modern pagans, it was not sufficiently great and noble, as
appears from his *Laws.* The seed of totalitarianism is sown here by
Plato:

> The Ruler of the universe has ordered all things with a view
> to the preservation and perfection of the whole; and each part has
> an appointed state of action and of being acted upon; and the
> smallest action or influence received affecting even the minutest
> fraction of the whole, has a presiding Minister.
> One of these portions of the universe is thine own, unhappy
> man, which, however little, is intended for the whole; and you do
> not seem to be aware that this and every creation is for the sake
> of the whole and that the life of the whole may be blessed; and
> that you are created for the sake of the whole, and the whole is not
> for the sake of you. For every physician and every skilled artist does
> all things for the sake of the whole, and not the whole for the
> sake of the part. You are annoyed because you do not see how that
> which is best for you is, as far as the laws of creation admit of this,
> best also for the universe.[13]

---

13 Bk. X, 903b, transl. B. Jowett.

8. Common Interests of the Mystical Body

Psychiatrists have encountered persons who are so emotionally upset that they are unable to see objects within a definite part of their normal field of vision, although their sight is normal. There is a strange spiritual astigmatism, not free from emotion, which is sometimes found in persons who otherwise have fine spiritual vision. This not unusual phenomenon can ever be observed in some who are more than ordinarily versed in spiritual science, who speculate subtly on controverted topics of ascetical and mystical theology and have more than ordinary devotion and austerity. And yet they seem unable to see, in their own case, the obvious duties of kindness and charity, especially in graciously yielding to another in opinion or project when the situation well allows it.

Only an insane person will drive a knife into his body. Christ has the same solicitous care for the members of His Mystical Body, as we have for our bodily members; "for no one ever hated his own flesh; on the contrary he nourishes and cherishes it, as Christ also does the Church" (Eph. 5:29). For this reason Christ wishes us to recognize Him, to acknowledge Him, and to show sincere love for Him in the members of His body. He is present in all men, even those who are not actually members of His body, since all men represent Christ to us.

Who is more a neighbor to Christ in me, than Christ in my neighbor? "Whom do you love least of all?" asks St. Francis de Sales; and he replies: "That is the degree in which you love Christ."

Christ loves his natural brethren intensely. He has become one of them and lived and died for them. But He loves His supernatural brethren ineffably more, loving them with a share of the paramount love which He has for Himself. "Christ also loved the Church, and delivered himself for her," is St. Paul's simple assertion (Eph. 5:25) of the mystery of God's love for His human creatures. It is natural that He should feel intensely whatever is done for or against His brethren.

The nature of the Mystical Body makes it clear that the interests
of Jesus in the members of His body are our interests, and that all
the members have in common the same interests, the same welfare,
the same happiness, and the same glory. A dead or sickly member of
the body of Christ should grieve us, as a withered member grieves
the other members of the human body, which seek with sympathetic
care to restore its vitality, just as Christ also loved the Church and
delivered himself up for her . . . in order that he might present to
himself the Church in all her glory . . . holy and without blemish
(Eph. 5:25–27).

St. Paul points out that the bodily members are not displeased
that another member functions very nobly and well; for instance,
the foot does not envy the eye, but rejoices and benefits in its perfection, because both belong to one and the same person. So the
Apostle enumerates some of the various gifts of the members of the
Mystical Body, which is one and the same mystical Person, as St.
Thomas calls it, in having one and the same life.

> But all these things [different activities of different members] are
> the work of one and the same Spirit, who divides to everyone
> according as he will. . . . For in one Spirit we all were baptized
> into one body . . . that there may be no disunion in the body, but
> that the members may have care for one another (1 Cor. 12:11–25).

He returns to the same unifying oneness of Christ in us, as the reason
for avoiding dissension and for furthering love among the Colos-
sians (3:9–11).

> Here [in the new Life of Christianity] there is not "Gentile and
> Jew," "circumcised and uncircumcised," "Barbarian and Scythian,"
> "slave and freeman," but Christ is all things and in all.

So clearly did M. Olier see, so intensely did he love our neighbor
Christ, that he bound himself by the vow of servitude, "which obliges
us so to love all the members of Jesus Christ, that we enter into their
interests and even prefer their interests to our own."[14] De Condren
took the same vow of servitude: "I give myself to God so that I
belong to all who come to me." He explains his understanding of

---

14 *Mémoires manuscrits*, Vol. II, col. 1102.

his vow thus: "Since I am the servant of all, everyone has a right to order me about."[15]

Love of neighbor is an obvious and obligatory means of paying in part our debt of love to God: "Beloved, if God so loved us, we ought also to love one another" (1 Jn. 4:11). We should be filled with joyful gratitude toward Christ, not only for the great benefits of redemption and grace arising from this close union with Him, but also because He has thus given us an opportunity to pay personally to Him in the person of others our pressing debt of love and affection. For, says St. Augustine:

> In Baptism, we have become not only Christians but Christ. Do you grasp, my brethren, this grace of God that has come upon us? We should be filled with wonder, we should exult with joy: we have become Christ, He the Head, we the members. He and we make the whole man.[16]

Fraternal charity, as intended by Christ, is the recognition and love of Him in our neighbor, who takes His place; or rather, our neighbor is the visible bearer of the invisible Christ in him. Our neighbor puts us in touch with Christ for several reasons. First, Christ made our neighbor His legal representative. But He is not absent from His representative. Christ is more present in him, receiving our treatment of him, than His representative is present to us.

Second, our neighbor is, through grace, Christ's fellow child of the Father and His brother and sister; He is present in our neighbor in grace as his very life.

Third, Christ gave His life for my neighbor.

Fourth, my neighbor is a member of the body of Christ, either in fact or in the intention of God. Thus we cannot affect the members without affecting the Head.

We cannot walk to God on the one foot of divine love; we must also use the other foot of fraternal love, or we do not go to Him. We are all "one in Christ." He wills to give Himself to us in His members. We cannot reject a part of Christ, our neighbor, one of His members, without rejecting the whole Christ. If, then, we wish to remain united with our Lord, we must be united with His members.

---

15 Amelotte, *Vie du P. Charles de Condren*, Vol. II, 21, 29, 33, 34.
16 *In Joan.* hom. 21:8, 9; *PL* 35, 1568.

As we must respect the whole person of a beloved one, so as not to injure any part of him, we must realize that we cannot have a warm love of Christ and at the same time be cold toward one of His brethren.

Life is fellowship. Lack of fellowship is equivalent to death. Heaven, too, is fellowship; and lack of it is hell. If we would be happy, so the maxim tells us, we must be tough with ourselves and tender with others. Because men form the mystical members of Christ's body, this maxim is for us a command, an imperative and indispensable means for our attaining happiness. Make God a stranger to man, and you make men strangers to one another.

When we have taken great pains as a doctor or nurse to cure a child, or when we have been generous of our time and efforts and interest in educating a child, conversation with the father of the child is cordial and friendly. If we are kind to our neighbor, we are assured of a loving reception when we speak to our neighbor's heavenly Father. Love of our Lord's brother and sister is the back door to His Sacred Heart, who readily overlooks our shortcomings. "Above all things, have a constant mutual charity among yourselves; for charity covers a multitude of sins" (1 Pet. 4:8). The thief said a kind word to our Lord, who not only forgave him all his thieving, but also allowed him to steal heaven.

Kindness is not sufficient without the religion promulgated by God become man; but religion cannot exist without kindness. We must do good to others as a part of our worship of God, and we must worship God partly in doing good to others. Kindness is one of the best tests of how deep our religion is. The deeper our religious faith that Christ is in our neighbor, the more our love for our fellow man approaches the instinctive love of the mother for her little child, who really is as concerned for the welfare and happiness of her child as she is for her own.

Charity is the proper preparation for worship. An increase of fraternal love is notably an increase of intimacy with God in prayer. From this we can well understand the deep significance of the emphatic direction of Christ that, in coming to God in worship, we must remove from our hearts enmity toward our brethren and His children. If we come to offer our sacrifice at the altar, He says, and realize that we are at enmity with our neighbor, while we seek to propitiate God with our offering: "leave there thy gift before the altar, and go first to be reconciled to thy brother; and then, come and offer thy gift" (Mt. 5:23). Christ bids us to leave Him at the altar, in order to seek Him in reconciliation with our brother.

St. John Chrysostom asserts that it is more Christ's desire that we take care of His poor than that we ornament His temple, which in itself he considers a grave duty:

> What is the use of loading Christ's altar with vessels of gold, if He Himself is dying of hunger? First satisfy His hunger; then adorn His altar. . . . Tell me, if you saw a man in need, even of the most necessary food and you should leave him standing there in order to set the table with dishes of gold [with no food], would he be thankful to you, or would he not be angry? And again, if you saw him clothed in rags and shivering with cold, and if, without giving any thought to his clothes, you were to erect columns of gold, telling him that all this were in his honor, would he not think you were mocking him and treating him with utmost contempt?
>
> But consider well that this is the way you treat Christ, when He goes about as a pilgrim and as a homeless wanderer; when instead of taking Him in, you embellish the floors and walls and capitals of columns [of His temple], and suspend lamps from silver chains. I am not saying this to criticize the use of such ornaments. We must attend to both, but to Christ first.[17]

9. Binocular Vision

To achieve our end, we must realize that we are not the center, motive, and purpose of the world about us. God's purpose is central; it alone supplies the ultimate reason for all that is. If we are unaware of His purpose, we can never perfectly grasp truth and beauty and worth and happiness. We must see things as God sees them. His all-wise interest, which must be our paramount interest, extends

---

[17] *Hom. in Matt.; PG* 58, 509.

equally to the welfare and happiness of others and to our own. Consequently, to put off the alluring falsity of distorted self-love and
take on the absolute truth of God's views, we must value and love
our neighbor just as we appreciate and love ourselves. "Love thy
neighbor as thyself" is the second essential principle of Christianity.

God values His human creatures as His children. They are the
work of His creation, and through the redemptive death of His Son
can be, in grace, sharers in His own divine nature and life. My
task is, as Paul reminds me, "to put on Christ," the self-sacrificing
Christ who again would live, in my life for my neighbor, and who
would be ready to die again, in my death for my neighbor.

So does the solidarity of Christianity demand the union of love
with our neighbor as the peremptory expression of our union of love
with God. Christ makes fraternal charity the sign by which we are
to be known as His true disciples: "By this will all men know that
you are my disciples, if you have love for one another" (Jn. 13:35).
All will know; there will be no mistaking a Christian. Christ is the
only one who asks His disciples to put their neighbor perfectly on
a level with themselves. He alone has made every man — Jew and
Samaritan, bond and free, rich and poor, friend and enemy — a
neighbor. He so sanctioned love of others, that He declared it to be
the extent of each man's love for Him: "As long as you did it for
one of these, the least of my brethren, you did it for me" (Mt. 25:40).

We can go to God only through Christ; and we cannot go through
Christ to God, unless we go through Christ in our neighbor. We
cannot be acceptable to God if we refuse to recognize His Son in
our neighbor. We cannot make exceptions to Christ in some of His
aspects and implications: "He is all lovely: such is my beloved"
(Cant. 5:16).

St. Augustine says:

> Brethren, our own two eyes do not see each other. One may say
> they do not know each other. But in the charity of the bodily
> frame, do they not know each other? It is clear that, in the charity
> which unites them together, they do know each other. For when
> both eyes open, the right eye may not rest on some object unless
> the left eye rests on it likewise. Direct, if you can, the glance of
> the right eye without the glance of the other. Together they meet

in one object; together they are directed to one object. Their aim is one.[18]

We cannot look on the all-desirable God with only the one eye of love of God in Himself; we must look at Him with binocular vision, which gives us our proper perspective; to see God correctly, we must also use the other eye of love of God in our neighbor.

10. Gauge of Divine Love

St. Teresa of Avila, the clear-seeing doctor of ascetical and mystical theology, sums up the life of sanctity in two ideas:

> . . . Here the Lord asks only two things of us: love for His Majesty and love for our neighbor. It is for these two virtues that we must strive; and if we attain them perfectly we are doing His will and so shall be united to Him. . . .
>
> The surest sign that we are keeping these two commandments is, I think, that we should really be loving our neighbor; for we cannot be sure if we are loving God, although we may have good reason for believing that we are, but we can know quite well if we are loving our neighbor. And be certain that the farther advanced you find you are in this, the greater the love you will have for God; for so dearly does His Majesty love us that He will reward our love for our neighbor by increasing the love which we bear to Himself, and that in a thousand ways: this I cannot doubt.
>
> It is most important that we should proceed in this matter very carefully; for if we have attained great perfection here, we have done everything. Our nature being so evil, I do not believe we could attain perfect love for our neighbor unless it had its roots in the love of God. . . . If you understand the importance of this virtue to us all, you would strive after nothing but gaining it . . . believe me, if you find you are lacking in this virtue, you have not yet attained union.[19]

This is, by no means, a new doctrine. It is only St. Teresa's correct understanding of St. John, the doctor of brotherly love, who is even clearer:

---

[18] *Tr. in Joan.* 6:10; *PL* 35, 2025.

[19] *Interior Castle* 5, 3; *The Complete Works of St. Teresa of Jesus*, transl. E. Allison Peers, from critical edition by P. Silverio de Santa Teresa, C.D., pp. 261–263 (New York: Sheed & Ward, 1949).

If anyone says "I love God," and hates his brother, he is a liar. For
how can he who does not love his brother, whom he sees, love
God, whom he does not see? And this commandment we have
from him, that he who loves God should love his brother also
(1 Jn. 4:20).

That is, if he does not love the visible representative of God, how
can he love the invisible God? The beloved Apostle gives the reason
for love of others:

Beloved, if God has so loved us, we also ought to love one another.
No one has ever seen God.

And he draws the conclusion that, since we cannot express our love
visibly to God, we should do so to His visible representative and
child, our neighbor:

If we love one another, God abides in us; and his love is perfected in us. In this we know that we abide in him and he in us,
because he has given us of his Spirit (ibid. 11–13).

It is notable fact that we cannot be really charitable out of Christian love of our neighbor and of God, and not merely for ulterior
motives, without being genuinely holy. In reverse, one cannot be
uncharitable, whatever else he may be, without being generally un-
holy. "Because iniquity will abound, the charity of the many will
grow cold" (Mt. 24:12), charity both toward God and toward the
neighbor, of which Christ had spoken shortly before (ibid. 22:37).
Hence, those religious congregations have chosen well which have
chosen charity to their neighbor as a principal work. Fraternal charity
is eminently sanctifying; for if we do good to Christ in our neighbor, Christ cannot fail to do great good to us by sanctifying us in
that union with Himself which He so desires and prays for. St. Paul,
who penetrated so deeply into the spirit of the Last Supper dis-
course of our Lord, faithfully echoes his Master's thought: "For
the whole Law is fulfilled in one word: Thou shalt love thy neighbor as thyself" (Gal. 5:14). Although the primary meaning of "law"
here, according to commentators, is the "social law," a number of
the early Fathers have made it include also the law of the love of
God. It may seem exaggerated to put such stress on love of one
another, but it does not seem so to St. Augustine:

Would you know if you are living the life of grace? if God is giving you His friendship? if you are numbered among Christ's disciples? if you are living by His Spirit? Question yourself. See if you love your neighbor for God, and you will have the answer; and that answer does not deceive.[20]

Again the great Bishop of Hippo says:

By what does one know that he has received the Holy Spirit? Let him question his heart. If he loves his brother, the Holy Spirit of God is in him. Let him see, let him prove himself before the eyes of God; let him see whether there is in him the love of peace and unity, the love of the Church diffused over the whole earth. Let him not rest content in loving the brother whom he has before his eyes; for we have many brethren whom we do not see; and in the unity of the Holy Spirit, we are joined to them. What difference that they are not with us? we are in one Body; we have one head in heaven. . . .

Then, if thou wouldst know if thou hast received the Holy Spirit, question thine heart. . . . If love of thy brethren be there, set thy mind at rest.[21]

The inspired John says the same, and even more forcibly than St. Paul:

We know that we have passed from [supernatural] death to life, because we love the brethren. He who does not love, abides in death (1 Jn. 3:14).

And he continues:

Beloved, let us love one another, for love is from God. And everyone who loves is born of God, and knows God. He who does not love does not know God; for God is love (*ibid.* 4:7–8).

It may be interesting to know what Henri Bergson, late Jewish French philosopher of note, who had come almost to the door of the Catholic Church, gathered from his long and close study of the Catholic mystics concerning fraternal charity. He tells us that the mystic, while apparently like other human beings, has been raised to a special rank of "partner of God," "helper of God," "receiving from God and giving to man":

---

20 *On the Letters of St. Paul,* tr. 6, c. 3.
21 *In Joan.* 6:10; *PL* 35, 2025.

The love which consumes him is no longer simply the love of his fellowman because of his love of God. It is the love of God [in him] for all men. Through God, and in the strength of God, he loves all mankind with a divine love.[22]

An absolutely certain sign of a group's nobility of living, of beautiful happiness, of remarkable, irreplaceable success, is the constant kindness which each member of the group places ahead of all other values of efficiency, rights, or other personal advantage. "Behold, how good and how pleasant it is for brethren to dwell together in unity" (Ps. 132:1). Those who have experience with vocations to the religious life well know how religious love of brethren is a lovely, fertile river which attracts multitudes. Says St. Augustine:

These same words of the Psalter, this sweet sound, that honeyed melody, as well of mind as of the hymn, did even beget monasteries. By this sound were stirred up the brethren who longed to dwell together. This verse was their trumpet. It sounded through the whole earth, and they who had been divided, were gathered together.[23]

Human experience has given rise to the sage proverb: Concord makes small powers grow mighty; discord disintegrates the greatest. For this fraternal charity, Christ made His always efficacious prayer for His Church, which, He said, was to accomplish greater works than the Apostles saw Him accomplish: "Holy Father, keep in Thy name those whom thou hast given me, that they may be one as we are" (Jn. 17:11).

Perfection of religious life is not easy; it is perfection of living in constant fraternal charity. Hence, Alvarez de Paz notes that even among religious — and this holds still more in the family and other groups — their most serious faults are against one another.[24] Certainly, the most effective dissolver of the bonds uniting the members of the Mystical Body is the acid of unkindness. A group in which there is never an unkind word is composed of supermen. Especially in groups of priests and religious, charity is the sole and infallible

---

22 *Les deux sources de la morale et de la religion*, 7 ed., 248–251.

23 *Ennar. in Ps.* 133, 2; trans. H. Walford, Oxford, 1857, v. 6, p. 110.

24 *De vita spir.* 3, 31.

test of spiritual greatness. "Love one another with fraternal charity, anticipating one another with honor" (Rom. 12:10).

It is a matter of experience that one person entering a group, by his or her infectious kindness, changes and elevates the whole group's tone and character, so that the relations of each member with the others are much more efficient, happier, and holier. In the generation of atomic power a rapidly mounting chain reaction is set up. A particle is injected into the group of particles of an atom's system, causing them, by a billiard-ball effect, to be similarly injected into other atom systems, which in turn do the same in geometric progression. This activity is considered the innermost heart of the power of the universe, which, when harnessed, can bring man unimagined material prosperity. The development of the power of fraternal love is a chain reaction of one person's kindness introduced into the systems of other lives, which in turn emit chain-reacting kindness into the systems of other lives, in geometric progression. This is the innermost exploitable power of the universe of human society, capable of developing a state of unimagined social health, happiness, and holiness.

11. A Ladder Must Have Two Ends

Christian love of neighbor is the ladder Jacob dreamed of, which rested on earth and went up into heaven. The object of brotherly love is a creature, but it joins us with the Creator, and by uniting us to His children it binds us to the loving Father. We cannot ascend to God by the ladder of love unless it rests on the love of neighbor; for it is the same love that produces acts of love of God and acts of love of neighbor. Our love, like the angels on Jacob's ladder, must go up and down: from God to our neighbor, from our neighbor to God.

St. Paul teaches that love of God is superior to all other gifts, and he describes it largely in terms of love of our neighbor:

> Charity is patient, is kind; charity does not envy, is not pretentious, is not puffed up, is not ambitious, is not self-seeking, is

not provoked; thinks no evil, does not rejoice over wickedness, but rejoices with the truth; bears with all things, believes all things, hopes all things, endures all things (1 Cor. 13:4–7).

The most elementary stage in the "illuminative way" is usually the light given by God to see the precious value of trials and crosses in ridding us of self and in "putting on Christ." Some would even pass for mystics who refuse to accept the ordinary inconveniences caused by their companions. They value only the trials which they think God Himself causes them interiorly, which they boastfully call their "dark night of the senses." Such an attitude is conclusive proof that their "mysticism" is spiritual tinsel. Our natural irritation at a necessary companionship with a person whose temperament jars on ours is a fairly good sign that we need to exercise the charity which such companionship demands.

There is a touchstone for the gold of love of neighbor. Is it penitential? There is no corporal penance comparable, either in worth or in severity, to the emotional penance of constant, perfect, loving human relations. "My greatest penance is common life," said St. John Berchmans; and we may rephrase his saying somewhat bluntly: our greatest penances are our companions, as every walk of life bears testimony. Do we have and show fraternal love for those who do not naturally attract us and who, because of their unattractive character, are most in need of our love? Yet all men are Christ's personal representatives. Does He not say: "You do it to me"?

Christ's love of His fellow man — intense, tender, self-sacrificing in the highest degree because it is His love of His Father — is the model of our love of man. "In all things let them see God; in all things let them seek God," two mottos of Loyola, should be the mottoes of love. They are well expressed in our Lord's prayer to His Father: "I pray for them . . . because they are thine" (Jn. 17:9). Every creature has a supreme claim to our affection in so far as it is God whom we love in loving any creature. Perhaps the subordination of love of neighbor to love of God may seem at first to make it impersonal and cold. Yet love of this kind is the warmest possible, giving rise to the tenderest care and to the most complete selflessness in our relations with others. It is only holy people who are really kind; others invariably determine, or at least modify and limit, their love of others by their own temporal interests.

False love of others is false love of ourselves. It is only when we love all creatures for God's sake that we love them all for their sakes and for our sakes. Right love is the root of all good. How little this is understood! St. John Chrysostom advises:

> Your own profit lies in the profit of your neighbor, and his in yours. As one who has his gold buried in the house of his neighbor . . . so likewise, he that will not seek his own profit in the advantage of his neighbor will not attain to rewards that are his own. God has so disposed our welfare that it must be bound with that of others. . . . We have been taught so to love our fellows that we regard as ours the good fortune our neighbor enjoys. Our fortune is in others. It is madness not to love them.[25]

St. Francis de Sales emphasizes this theme, common with writers of the Church since the time of our Lord:

> Since man is "created to the image and likeness of God," so God has ordained that we should love our fellowman with a love that is the image and likeness of our love of God. . . . The likeness of love of God with the love of our neighbor is the identical reason for both loves: the infinite Good that God is; for an image of God's perfection should be loved for what it represents. Hence, the creature is not loved only for itself. Thus, in fact, the ultimate object, which we love in both love of God and of man, is the same: God's infinite Goodness.[26]

True service of man is service of God. But this motto has been transposed by millions, for whom God has become implicitly or explicitly the synonym for society, so as to read: All service of God is service of man. The only sin, then, for such a religion, the only infraction of such law is a sin and offense against society; for in such a view of human life the only responsibility is responsibility to society. Thus for millions who have very little definite and exact belief, religion has become wholly social service. They have only one end to the ladder of their lives. Moreover, for such persons there is no spiritual soul in man, and consequently no future life; and their philanthropy has as its sole purpose the material betterment of

---

25 *In 1 Cor.* 13:4; hom. 33; *PG* 57, 280.
26 *The Love of God,* 10, 1.

man, for instance, by diminishing poverty and sickness.

While there is the material element in man, he needs material charity; and there is in this regard no record comparable to that of the Church which dedicates millions of her children's whole lives to assuage the material sufferings of humanity of every race, color, and religion. But by its very etymology, "tenderness," charity is rather a subjective spiritual giving of interior love to another, rather an attitude of spiritual benevolence to a spiritual being, than a giving of material aid to another being of matter.

So pressing is our Lord's insistence on fraternal love as our love for Him, that it is plainly His pleasure that, in doubt about precedence in a conflict of duties, we should give the preference to love of others. Charity toward others had precedence when He cured the sick on the Sabbath, to the insincere scandal of the Pharisees who, as He pointedly observed, were quite ready to be kind on the Sabbath to a floundering ass that had fallen into a deep ditch, but not toward a suffering human child of God.

As we have daily natural food for our natural human life, so we have daily supernatural food for our supernatural life, which exteriorly is largely love of our neighbor. St. Paul calls the Eucharist the *Agape*, the Love Feast, the bond of union between the members of Christ's Mystical Body: "For we, being many, are one bread, one body, all that partake of the one bread" (1 Cor. 10:17). St. Cyril of Alexandria, with many other teachers of all ages of the Church, explains that the Eucharist is the table that unites the family of the children of God, in fulfillment of our Lord's prayer at the first Eucharist: "that they may be all one in Us."

> As in the Eucharist we are all united with the same Humanity, so we are all united with one another. . . . In order that we might strive for union with God and among ourselves and might be fused into one, the Only-begotten excogitated a way through the Wisdom proper in Him and through the counsel of the Father. By His one Eucharistic Humanity blessing those belonging in Him, He made them one body with Himself and with one another. Who will separate them from their physical union among themselves, when they have been joined with the one holy Humanity, into unity with Christ?[27]

---

[27] *In Joan.* 11, 11; *PG* 74, 560.

Characteristically, in his vivid manner, Chrysostom looks on the Eucharist as the love feast of Christians:

> The Father, desirous of bringing us to a tender mutual affection, has devised that we should drink out of one cup . . . a mark of intense love. We have shared a spiritual table; let us also share a spiritual love.
>
> For if brigands in sharing food forget their characteristic trait [of cruelty], what excuse have we who repeatedly partake together of the Lord's Body, and yet do not imitate the brigands' mildness. For many, not even a common table but merely being of the same city, is sufficient reason for friendship. And we, when we have the same city and house, and table and way and door and root and Life and Head and King and teacher and judge and Maker and Father, and all things in common — what indulgence can we deserve if we be divided from one another?[28]

---

[28] *In Rom.* hom. 8, c. 4.

II. SOME CHARACTERISTICS OF FRATERNAL CHARITY

1. Deep, Wide, Delicate, and Constant

This love of Christ in all our love of others, this love of all others "in Christ," is the sole explanation of the intensity, universality, unwavering constancy, and minute delicacy of fraternal charity. Fortunate are we that fraternal love is for the sake of the infinite worth of Christ, and not for the sake of our sometimes very limited worth. If we love others for their own sakes, we love them for their own worth; and their worth, at best, is very little, while many of us have so little worth for others that we would not excite a great degree of love in any, and would excite no love whatever in most of our neighbors. The intensity of our love of Christ in our love of others stimulates us to a sacrifice of self and to a tenderness for which purely personal motives would be altogether insufficient. As St. Francis de Sales attested in his own case to St. Frances de Chantal:

> My dear daughter, it seems to me now that everything is nothing except in God, in whom, nevertheless, and for whom, I love much more tenderly those whom I love.[1]

Because He is divine, Christ, the perfect man, is so grandly human. Not only, like Shakespeare, does He describe universal humanity with photographic clearness; not only, as the sage, or as all sages together, does He teach the wisdom of universal humanity; He is not merely the model of perfection for universal humanity; He *is* the life and love participated in all humanity, which, as it should be, is supernatural. Above all, He is the reason of all that deserves love in

---

[1] *Lettres de St. Francois de Sales,* Paris, 1758, n. 799.

universal humanity. His noble person is fit and is intended to set all human hearts of all ages and all races vibrating in symphonic harmony. His wise love is the philosopher's wisdom for the restless questioning mind of man. His unifying love is meant to bind together all the human loves, which, without His love in them, so generally involve enmities.

Nationalism, racism, bigotry, or any other kind of sectionalism, by which we dislike any group, is opposed to our common nature and to the common Christ indwelling, or at least represented, in all humanity. Strangers are only friends whom we do not know. The soldier must love the enemy he shoots, just as the executioner must love the criminal he executes. The perfectly kindly person is able to say with Belloc, in his Christmas carol in "The Four Men":

> May all my enemies go to hell!
> Noel! Noel! Noel! Noel!

because he holds his only enemies to be sin and Satan.

Catholic in His mission, and catholic in His heart, Christ founded and still lives in a catholic religion; and all who are not shallow-minded and shallow-hearted cannot but recognize the catholicity of Christ and conform themselves and their views and their loves therewith, as "other Christs," by the catholicity of their love. Transcendent as God, Christ transcends the borders of nationality and the borders of social grades. If we allow ourselves to be hemmed in by sectionalism, we cannot but shut out Christ in those we do not love. Science and art are said to be universal, restricted to no group. Grace, the basis of supernatural fraternal love, immeasurably more than science and art, knows no boundaries, no races, no educational degrees, no levels in society, no wealth or power. All human beings are God's natural or supernatural children; and if we love God, we must say to Him the words of Ruth (1:16): "Thy people are my people."

St. James points out that a Christian is not a snob:

My brethren, do not join faith in our glorious Lord Jesus Christ to partiality towards persons. For if a man in fine apparel, having a gold ring, enters your assembly, and a poor man in mean attire enters also, and you pay attention to him who is clothed in fine apparel and say, "Sit thou here in this good place"; but you say to the poor man, "Stand thou there," or, "Sit by my footstool"; are you not making distinctions among yourselves, and do you not become judges with evil thoughts? (2:1–4.)

Manifold is the application of St. Augustine's dictum: "Let no one excuse himself [from love of others] by love of some."[2] Pagan Greeks and Romans, like later and modern pagans, who lauded love so highly, generally meant love of one or of a few. Those who taught love of all men, like Seneca, were exceedingly rare; and the practice was rarer, or rather, nonexistent. Apart from God, the Father-Creator of all mankind, they simply had no reason why they should love all men of all nations, civilized and uncivilized, men of all characters, good and bad, men of all dispositions toward us, friendly and inimical. Who but God ever taught: "Love your enemies, do good to those who hate you"? And God's reason is Himself: "so that you may be children of your Father in heaven" (Mt. 5:44, 45).

With what divine tenderness and divine wisdom, Christ has arranged for the protection of the weak and the unfortunate among His brethren! He has placed Himself between them and the egoistic, self-centered tendencies of the strong and fortunate. We cannot touch them without touching Christ. If that touch is harsh, it is first harsh toward Him. Paul who heard these words of the Head protesting for His members: "Why persecutest thou Me?" never ends exhorting his Christians to love Christ in His brethren.

Because of the eternal Christ in our brother, St. Martin was given to see Christ clad in half of his own mantle, which he had given to a beggar the day before. For this reason, the angry husband of St. Elizabeth of Hungary could see the form of Christ in place of the leper whom she had taken into her house and cared for. For this reason, Christ claims a never changing reverence and love for all the members of His Mystical Body.

Chrysostom comments:

Do you see what a wall He has set around them, and what earnest care He takes of those that are contemptible and perishing? He threatens irremediable ills for them who make them fall. He promises great blessings for them who show them great care and attention. He recalls once more His own example and that of His

---

[2] *In Epist. ad Parthos*, 10; *PL* 35, 2056.

Father. Let us also imitate Him, refusing none of the tasks that seem lowly and troublesome, for our brother's sake. Though we have to serve him, though he be lowly, though he be mean, upon whom we must wait, though the work be laborious, though we must cross mountains and precipices, let all be held endurable for the salvation of our brother. For a soul is of such earnest care to God that, for him, He spared not His own Son. "As long as you did it to one of these least of my brethren, You did it to Me" (Mt. 25:40). . . . For this reason they are Thy brethren, because they are lowly, because they are poor, because they are outcast. . . . These are the ones He invites most of all to be His brethren: the unknown, the despised. . . .³

Love of neighbor, like love of God, is delicate and minute in its manifestation. There is a mistake easily made, in the aspiration to great fraternal love, of waiting for great and notable opportunities for the manifestation of that love in a more or less heroic degree. Life does not consist of heroics; in fact, heroics could be totally absent from a full and perfect life of love. The love "that contemneth small things shall fall by little by little" (Ecclus. 19:1).

Love is the business of living and must be in constant effect in the tiny events of every day, just as the ordinary person's business transactions are usually in small amounts: small purchases of clothes, groceries, furniture, carfare, fuel, and such items, just because life is made up of such small things for the average man. Kindness has been called the small coins of love. "The kindest man," says Shakespeare, is "the best-conditioned and unwearied spirit in doing courtesies."⁴

Most of us must express love, not in great, but in small self-sacrifices; not in notable, but in little unnoticed victories over emotions which are interwoven into the warp and woof of the fabric of our lives. It is only the small threads of small kindnesses that can weave the mantle of the cloth of love, which at once covers us with beauty and others with protection.

We need not give thought to great exploits and sacrifices of charity, if we are attentive to the small, easily neglected signs and self-restraints of kindness. Moreover, it is the unintermittent delicacies

³ *In Mt.* 8:10; *PG* 58, 580.
⁴ *Merchant of Venice*, 3, 2, 295.

of kindness which give occasional great love its value; and vice
versa, the life which is not made up of minute acts and sacrifices of
feeling is not a kind life. To the lack of constant little efforts of
affability and graciousness in routine personal contact, we can apply
the words of G. Massey ("Our Wee White Rose"):

> You scarce could think so small a thing
> Could leave a loss so large.

Living must be a flowing river of love, which, to carry us, to
refresh us, charm us with its beauty, must be a connected flow of
drops. A freshet in the spring and a dry bed in the summer make a
poor river. Life is flow, *"panta rei,"* said the old Greek philosopher.
Love must be a continued, uninterrupted flow, if it would be in
accord with our fluent life. It is hardly satisfactory to our fellow
that, arroyo-like, we deluge him for a brief time with kindness, and
thereafter totally dry up. "Love of our neighbor," says Origen, "is
a debt that we must pay every day."[5]

For the pagan, the gods, because they are of human though magnified stature, cannot be concerned with small things, are "careless
of mankind." For the Christian, God, because He is infinite, must
be concerned with the smallest human things, as He is with the
greatest. The actions affecting Christ in His representative or member of His Body, and the kindness done through Christ in them
cannot be small, for it is "in Christ," the infinite Word, and no
action "in Christ" is small.

The chief anxiety of human love and friendship is that it be
constant, permanent, and secure. Time inevitably brings change in
all things of earth, for the very definition of time is sequence of
changes. There is nothing constant in this world but inconstancy.
Time makes circles out of squares, as Horace tells; and with time,
either friendship disappears, or the reason for friendship, or the
friend. If we love others for what they are or have, both easily
change, and our stream of love dries up, as its source dries up. But
if we love others because of the Christ in them, our love will be as
"Jesus Christ is the same, yesterday and today, yes, and forever"
(Hebr. 13:8).

---

[5] *In Rom.* 9:30.

2. Frame of the Masterpiece

Our neighbor is the frame of the divine masterpiece, Christ. The love of our neighbor is the setting of our love of God. We must not fix our consideration exclusively on the nature of the frame, whether our neighbor be of this or of that appearance, influential or insignificant, cultured or lacking in social graces, or even whether he be an enemy or friend. We must admire the beauty, graciousness, wealth, and greatness of Christ, the masterpiece enframed in him. In fact, "the more insignificant thy brother is," observes St. John Chrysostom, "the more Christ comes to you in him."[6]

If, in one of the great art galleries, you were to offer to replace, with a frame of solid gold, a frame on one of the pictures of a master painter, no matter how roughly time had handled it, you could not have the original frame replaced; for it is the frame that the master deemed best suited for his painting. Our neighbor, with his perhaps very limited qualities of human character and ability, is the frame which the divine Master judged best to represent Himself to us. We should respect His infinitely artistic judgment and not belittle Christ's "little ones," after the fashion of decadent artists who replaced, by flamboyant rococo frames, the original frames of the sincere paintings of the pre-Raphaelite age.

St. Catherine of Siena was exceptionally beautiful; and among her charms, was a head of unusual golden hair. Her family wished her to marry one of the wealthy young blades of Siena who besieged her for her hand. Such an alliance would materially aid the finances of her honorable, but not rich, Benincasa family. Catherine, however, had other ideas; she had vowed her virginity to Christ and wished to become a religious. At length, after a long conflict with her emotions, she took the decided step of secretly cutting off her fair tresses, so much admired, and placed a kerchief over her head, in the fashion of Italian women, in order to conceal the fact from the family. Lapa, her matter-of-fact and hot-tempered mother,

---

[6] *In Acta Ap.*, hom, 45; *PG* 60, 318.

who was ruler of the family, was not long in finding it strange that
Catherine kept the kerchief on her head with such care; and she
soon uncovered the shorn head.

A stormy hour followed the discovery. The family was furious and
heaped reproaches on her. Lapa, with all the eloquence of her
versatile tongue, and with all the powers of her much-exercised
lungs, vowed that she would force Catherine to marry: "Your hair
will grow again; and you marry, if it kills you!" A council of the
elder children of the family was called by Lapa, at which the mild-
mannered father was present, and she decreed that Catherine would
no longer have a room for herself in which she could indulge in
her pious follies. Moreover, the housemaid was discharged and
Catherine was sentenced to take her place. In order to wear down
her patience, she was treated meanly, so that she would be forced
to escape from her servitude into marriage.

To support this trial Catherine had recourse to the artifice of
picturing her home as Nazareth, in which she served our Lord and
His Mother and Joseph and the disciples. Her beloved father, gentle
and pious, represented St. Joseph. Her mother, Lapa, was, as well as
she could be, the Blessed Virgin; while the other members of the
family were our Lord's disciples. In all, she was serving her Master,
her heavenly spouse; and so, in His service, she hurried all day long,
up and down the long and narrow stair from the lower room on
the side of a hill to the upper rooms. It was always His voice that
she heard calling her in the voices of the others. She cooked for Him
and served Him at His table. Her device wore down the opposition;
and finally the family surrendered to her desires.[7]

It is no imagination, but the realest of facts, that I live, labor, and
suffer for Christ in those about me. This consciousness of my dealing
with Christ in others should not only support me in my difficulties
with them, but it should also develop in me sincerest courtesy,
unselfishness, and enthusiasm toward any and everyone.

St. Augustine gives vent to his feeling for Christ in his brethren
through that beautiful passage on the Psalms, of which this is
a part:

Still Christ is in want; still Christ is a wanderer. Still Christ is ill;

---

[7] Cf. Jorgenson, *St. Catherine of Siena*, transl. I. Lund, Longmans, c. IV.

still Christ is in prison; and we injure Him unless He can say to us: "I was hungry and you gave Me to eat; I thirsted and you gave Me to drink. I was a stranger and you received Me; sick, and you visited Me."[8]

There is no hunger and thirst like that of the heart hungering and thirsting to be loved, to be noticed, to be esteemed by one's fellows. There is no stranger so lonely as the stranger to love and concern. There is no sickness like that of the sick heart. It is not so much our material food, drink, shelter, or medicine for which others long; it is our loving attitude that is food and drink and shelter and medicine to them.

The following "Irish Blessing" asks for compassion, the great wealth which enriches us by our giving it to others:

> May the light shine out of the two eyes of you,
> like a candle set in two windows of a house,
> bidding the wanderer to come in out of the storm.

3. *"Pity at Home"*

Reason, perceiving God's will for my individual nature in its relations to others, demands that I have more "pity at home" than for someone at the antipodes.

Our neighbor, according to the etymology of the word, is the "nigh boor" to us, whoever and whatever he may be. The more he is "nigh" to us the more he is our neighbor; and just so, the more he is a "boor." When Christ asked us to love our neighbor as ourselves, He did not mean — as we are apt to propose to ourselves — that we are to be kind to especially amiable and gifted or especially unfortunate and needy persons. He meant precisely the "one nigh to us." "Let these first learn to provide for their own household" is St. Paul's realistic teaching (1 Tim. 5:4). We are to show our love to others in proportion to their proximity.

The members of the Mystical Body are to be most constantly kind and considerate toward the members closest to them. Hence, rela-

---

[8] *Ennar. in Ps.* 136, n. 5; *PL* 37, 1105.

tives and those with whom Providence has located our lives are to
be the object of greater study in the realization of our love of
Christ. Other things being equal, our business associates are more our
neighbors than the occasional customer; family members are more
our neighbors than business associates; the religious of a house are
more neighbors than those of their family; religious or business
people, who are continually in contact with us, are more our neighbors than those of the same group who are less intimately and less
constantly dealing with us. Families need mutual love more than
they need an automobile, or even a house, food, and clothing. A
family can be a perfect family, even though it lacks necessities
in nutrition and housing; but it cannot have a tolerable family life,
whatever its material appointments, without love.

The person who is an insufferable bear with his family or em-
ployees, while exuding honey with those above him or with a customer, is hardly living according to the principle of proximity in
his fraternal charity. We must not forget that there is a moral
proximity, as well as a physical proximity, in the diffusion of our
love. In equal settings, parents, superiors, relatives, benefactors,
friends, should have prior rank in the disbursing of our love. Intimacy of neighborliness should lead us not only to do more frequent
acts of kindness, but also to forget the inevitable, and not infre-
quent, jolt to our feelings received from those who are so near to
us that sometimes they come too near. Often more valuable than a
good memory is a good forgetter.

Perhaps the easiest understood and the most effective, though somewhat unusual, rule of perfection in fraternal love is to study how I
can make everyone in my group really like me. Seemingly a selfish
rule, this is only Christ's rule seen from the other fellow's viewpoint;
for the only way to make myself generally liked is to be kind to all
others. If we propose to be kind to every one of our daily companions, we may not see how to carry out this resolution. If we
set, as our ideal, to be liked by everyone about us, we immediately
know how we are to act and speak. We see clearly then that we
must please others as they wish to be pleased, not as we think they
ought to be pleased. We study their likes and dislikes. We perform

the heroic penances of daylong, lifelong adaptation to their likes and dislikes, unless, of course, a greater obligation demands otherwise. But very rarely will we fail to make ourselves liked, that is, make our love acceptable to others, by tactfulness.

This wise and constant subjection of ourselves and our likes to others and to their likes is not only a very unusual and high degree of Christlike living; it is also, as it should be, the greatest degree of efficiency and success in life. The most perfect practice of the spiritual life should, and does normally, lead to the greatest possible success and happiness. It is when we are unkind in protecting our sensitive "rights" that our rights are least secure. Worship of the god Efficiency, without human allowance for the deficiencies of those with whom we deal, makes our lives most inefficient, and even sometimes, as experience shows, it wrecks us totally. Gentle subjection at times to the unreasonableness of others is a powerful rule over mankind, as it was in the case of Him who "was subject to them."

Great perfection demands a lifelong study. The knowledge of practical psychology needed for perfection in charity is unlimited, and not by any means proportionate to the theoretical book knowledge of psychology. Not an academic degree, but a high degree in the practical wisdom taught by Him who is Love is needed to react perfectly to the myriad intricacies of human feelings, expressed by all our associates in their words and actions. The persons with whom we are to be kind are continually changing; and we must institute ever new studies of the likes and dislikes of new associates — not to speak of the constant change taking place in the same person.

The ideal of kindness is not merely, nor principally, the negative avoidance of offense, which very many think of when there is question of being kind. The positive perfecting of kindly, wise, tactful speech and action should be our chief care in the study of charity toward others, rather than the removal of unkindness from our words and behavior. Positive charity is limitless in its possibilities, and it amply attends to the negative correction of uncharitable faults.

In all our study of the human characters about us, and in all our firm proposals to enrich our lives with the kindliness of Christ, we must be aware that our undertaking is not a mere psychological or

ethical one, but also a supernatural development for which alone
grace suffices, and for which we must constantly pray. There is only
one greater gift for which we should pray: the love of God, which
is expressed socially in fraternal love; and for the acquisition of perfection in fraternal love we need an abundance of all the gifts of
the Holy Spirit of love. We cannot, therefore, pray too much for
that virtue which is so essential to the Christ-life; and praying for
it, we are praying for others who are its beneficiaries.

The Mystical Body, through grace, is a real union, not merely a
moral union, or union of purpose, inasmuch as the Holy Spirit, the
bond of love, is real, one and the same, in each distinct member.
Christians should build up in their mind and will the virtue of
charitable union to correspond to this corporate union of their
beings. The Mystical Body is a union of life; hence, it should be
developed as union of thought and feeling and will, which are the
essentials of human life.

Our rejection of Christ, in major or minor degree, by our unkindness toward Him in others, results invariably from our over-
evaluation of something else — our rights, for instance, or our efficiency, or our good name, economy, or pleasure. All the while, we
are stupidly unaware of losing, by our conduct, the very values which
we seek. As good gamblers, we must be ready to lose minor values in
order to gain far greater spiritual values in the long run. "Lose that
thou mayest gain; die that thou mayest live." "Strive after the
greater gifts" (1 Cor. 12:31). How often we have lost spiritual
fortunes because we were unable to say, at the prospect of gaining
some minor value instead, "It's not worth it!"

Probably more than half of our required exercise of charity is in
the gentle acceptance of the disagreeable. Like union with God's
will in general, love of neighbor is both active and passive. And, as
in conformity with God's will, the passive phase of kindness is more
difficult, more important, and more sanctifying.

Deliberate planning is necessary to preserve kindly harmony of
spirit in a permanent group. We must have an enduring awareness
of the pleasure of our associates if we would get along with the
people we can't get along without. Every day there must be studied,

as well as spontaneous, expressions of affection. A regulated, recurring act of kindness is as healthy as the regular airing of a room.

Unkindness is never the right solution of a conflict of interests or feelings. It's an attempt at emotional escape, when opposition should be solved positively or absorbed by kindly patience; and the problem always follows us in our vain escape, but magnified and multiplied. Anything is a better solution of domestic and group conflicts than unkindness. Outrageous blunders, unreasonable emotions, even perverse injury are not remedied by more unkindness from the injured party. Two evils do not make a good. Only inexhaustible tolerance and boundless forgiveness will produce the happiness possible in a given social situation, and at the same time greater holiness. We destroy our enemies most effectively and satisfactorily when we make them our friends by returning them love for their hate.

4. Charity and Truth

Christ's fervent wish and prayer, as He was about to consummate His mission on earth, was that we might be closely united in love of one another through union with the Trinity in one great Body:

> . . . that all may be one, even as thou, Father, in me and I in thee; that they also may be one in us; that the world may believe that thou hast sent me (Jn. 17:21).

Our Lord sought this intimate union among us in order that our love for our fellows should be a proof of His messianic mission from the Father and of the religion He taught. The truth of Christianity is established by reasoning and faith, not by mere emotion. Christ appealed to the intellect when He proposed His miracles as the evidence of His supernatural mission from the Father. However, if Christianity is religion for the whole man, in which to glorify God by the perfection of his humanity, then it must bring man, through grace, to the height of emotional perfection: to the highest possible reach of love for one's neighbor. A supernatural religion must be a religion of supernatural social love reflecting the society of the Trinity.

True philosophy of man culminates in brotherly love, for the reason that man, the child of God, is meant to be loved by the other children of the Creator. This was the factual result of Christianity to which the pagans gave admiring testimony. It was unbelievable for pagans, with all their material civilization, to see rich men really love the poor or a free man really love a slave, who was considered a beast of burden. Least of all could they accept love of enemies who calumniated and persecuted them.

Love of one's fellows, is not, indeed, *all* truth; but it is so great a part of truth, that, where men see it, they are often ready to accept unquestioningly any error or inconsistency associated with it. Wherever there is true religion, true Christianity, there is love of all mankind. But it is not always true that wherever there is this love, there is true religion in its fullness without serious error. In this sense, the fact of Christian unity in love is a proof of Christ's divine mission; namely, that, if He came from God, His philosophy of life must result in the great boon and happiness of mankind united in love.

We associate love with truth to such an extent that it is a very natural mistake to take for granted that love always is the whole truth, when it may be only partial and deficient truth. There can be no truth that does not mean love. Thus it comes to pass that generous and self-sacrificing corporal and spiritual works of mercy practiced by defective religions are often all that is needed to lead both educated and uneducated to embrace, without sufficient examination, the tenets of those religions. On the other hand, some of those who have the true religion of Christ and are members of His Mystical Body, are under the merited lash which Swift lays on: "We have enough religion to make us hate, but not enough to love one another."[9] It is a pity that, while the Church as a Body is filled with Christ's love of the neighbor, many individual Catholics do not propagandize their Catholic faith by their kindness.

Deeply in accord with human nature, fraternal charity nevertheless requires a supernatural and divine religion for its constant and full exercise. Many pagan philosophers, both ancient and modern, glimpse

---

[9] *Spectator,* n. 459.

the beauty and magnificence of the palace of universal love in which man is supposed to dwell. For them, it is only a wishful mirage; they cannot build it; and if they build it, they have not the motivation to induce mankind to live in it, leaving their discordant hates, domestic, political, religious, and racist, outside its doors. Such were the Stoic teachers whose moral philosophy was admired, but practiced constantly by hardly anybody.

Our fraternal charity not only opens the eyes of the pagan to see the truth that Christ's religion is necessary for human nature but it also clears the mind of the Christian of the darkness of selfishness so that he can see God better. It is a psychological fact that the kindly person's mind is clearer for its kindliness. It is a supernatural fact that the greater the indwelling of the kindly Christ in us through grace, because of our increasing kindliness, the greater our participation in His own vision of God, both now and in eternity. St. Augustine holds that love of neighbor is a necessary purge of our eyes in order to see God:

> As you do not yet see God, you earn the sight of Him by loving your neighbor. By fraternal love, you purge your eye for seeing God: "If thou lovest not thy neighbor, whom thou seest, how canst thou love God whom thou dost not see?" (1 Jn. 4:20.)
> If you say to me: Show me God that I may love Him, what shall I answer but what the same John says (*ibid.*): "No man hath seen God at any time." . . . Look at the source of the love of your neighbor; and there you will see, as you can, God.[10]

Onto the human motives for charity Christ heaped the divine motives of grace, supernatural union with Him and with the Trinity, supernatural glory to God, supernatural happiness in sharing His own happiness — motives more than ample to lead reasonable beings to enter and live in the grand and blissful palace of charity. Of course, there are no motives which can force man's free choice not to follow inhuman hate against the clearest reason and against his own true welfare. Thus it is that Christians who have these more than valid reasons for charity, and who thus have greater obligation, not infrequently disregard them or do not follow them with the perfection they well demand.

---

[10] *In Joan.*, tr. 17, n. 8.

5. Hate

God has seen to it, by giving us a spontaneous instinct of self-preservation, that we cannot wish evil, as evil, upon ourselves. He has also willed that we freely wish others well in the same way that we wish well to ourselves. It is diabolical to wish evil to God; and, as love of our neighbor is one of the provinces of the love of God, it is diabolical, as well as inhuman, to hate our neighbor. C. S. Lewis pictures the psychologist devil, Screwtape, as advising a minor devil: "We know that He [God] cannot love; nobody can; it doesn't make sense."[11] St. Teresa gave a psychological definition of Satan: "He who does not love."

The human spirit that is ruled by hate is unhappy, unreasonable, and abnormal. No one can carry a grudge for long and not have it balefully affect his character and nerves. Hate is a cannon that kills the gunner, a principle of self-destruction, as well as destruction of others and of God's glory. It is a negativistic means of acquiring or preserving some value; but negativistic, it does not produce, it only destroys.

"Gold begets in brethren hate," says the poet Cowley. Short is the road from the dwelling of Fear or of Envy to the dwelling of Hate. Seneca shrewdly notes the perversity of hate: "We by no means always injure others because we hate them; often we hate others because we have injured them."[12] In more than one way, "He who hates his brother is in the darkness, and walks in the darkness, and he does not know whither he goes, because the darkness has blinded his eyes" (1 Jn. 2:11).

Philosophies, politics, and religions based on hatred of some groups of mankind are *ipso facto* false, and like all falsity are antihuman and anti-God, who, as a social being, made a social creation of which man is naturally the most social being on earth. Hatred between classes in Communist sociology is ample proof that this is a disastrous

---

11 *The Screwtape Letters* (New York: Macmillan, 1943), p. 98.
12 *On Anger*, 2:33.

St. John Chrysostom expresses his wonder in a similar way:

What is more wonderful than this? Those who crucified him and conspired to kill him, after they crucify him, are made the children of God.[18]

Again, in another sermon, Augustine peers into the depths of the love of the Sacred Heart for even his enemies:

When hanging on the cross he prayed. He saw and foresaw all his enemies; but he foresaw that many of them would become friends. Thus he begged pardon for all. They were furious; he prayed. They said to Pilate: "Crucify him!" He cried out: "Father, forgive them!" He hung on the harsh nails; but he did not lose his mildness. He asked pardon from them from whom he received such injury. . . . Finally, after the resurrection, he cured those madmen, whom he tolerated while hanging on the cross; and those believers drank his blood which he had shed.[19]

St. Paul tells us that by dying for all men, the Redeemer broke down the wall of enmity between both Jews and gentiles and between them and God, making all men one fold of mutual love, of which He is the loving Shepherd. Those, he says, who "were once afar off, have been brought near through the blood of Christ," reconciled to God "by the cross having slain the enmity in himself" (Eph. 2:13–17).

God does not will evil to us because of our disregard of His infinite rights. "Is it my will that a sinner should die," saith the Lord, "and not that he be converted from his ways, and live?" (Ezech. 18:23.) If so, He rightly asks us to dispel our enmities toward His other children, for He has forgiven us greater crimes than we are called upon to forgive in others. In fact, the injuries to our rights, which God is ready to forgive our neighbors, are immeasurably greater injuries to His rights.

The Sacred Heart was well aware always, but especially at the Last Supper, of the future betrayal of the Apostles; yet, full of love for them, He expressed it most sublimely in words, and still more sublimely in giving them His love feast, His agape, before He died for them.

---

[18] In Matt. 79; PG 58, 721.
[19] Serm. 382, 2; PL 39, 1685.

theory, for it is unnatural to man. Goethe, unconsciously condemning his own country's future Nazi racial hatred, noted the obvious truth: "National hatred is something peculiar. You will always find it strongest and most violent where there is the lowest degree of culture."[13] Lenin would distort human nature through hate, in order to make it fit into the violence of Sovietism:

We must hate. Hate is the basis of Communism. Children must be taught to hate their parents, if they are not communists.[14]

Sadly, this principle is not held as mere theory in Russia today. The Minister of Russian Public Education expounds to his people the principles of Soviet sociology according to its basic Marxian philosophy which should be the spirit of Russian life and action. They are the principles of Satan, whom Milton describes as "immortal hate."

We hate Christianity and the Christians; even the best of them must be regarded as our worst enemies. They preach love of one's neighbor and mercy, which is contrary to our principle. Down with love of our neighbor! What we need is hatred. We must know how to hate. Only thus shall we conquer the universe.[15]

A variation of hatred is resentment. Suppose we had a stroke of amnesia immediately after experiencing an outrageous injustice. Would it cause us suffering any longer? With a cherished grievance, we are like a kitten which so entangles itself in a ball of yarn that it can hardly move. Our resentment rolls the injury over and over in our bitter spirit, day after day, year after year, until we are totally entangled in depression and self-pity, helpless and unable to enjoy normal emotions.

God never intended us to suffer nearly as much pain of heart as we cause ourselves. It is almost a general truth that we ourselves, by our irrational and unspiritual reaction to unpleasant experiences, are the real cause of our sufferings. No one can, in general, make us really unhappy but ourselves. Many a married life is a shambles because of the refusal to rise above pique and sulkiness over injured feelings.

---

[13] Conversations with Echermann.
[14] Speech to Commissars of Education, 1923.
[15] Cf. E. J. Walsh, S.J., Why Pope Pius XI Asked Prayers for Russia, Catholic Near East Welfare Assn., N. Y., 1930, pp. 4–5.

Christ certainly advised us to "seek the things that are for our peace," as well as for God's glory and the good of our neighbor. No psychology can be as sound as His, whether on the natural or supernatural plane. Why keep forever tearing open the wound of injustice? Why keep on tasting the gall of humiliation? Ask yourself: "Does such a mentality do me or anyone else any good?" Someone appears superior to us. Do we better the situation, even for ourselves, by an attitude of destructive jealousy? "I'll take him [or her] down a peg!" And when we have accomplished our vicious intent, we have only bedeviled our world.

Enormous is the cost of continued hurt feelings — spiritual, social, emotional, physical. Physicians know well that prolonged resentment is often the hidden cause of indigestion, insomnia, and abnormal fatigue. It is an efficient method for creating high blood pressure and for developing or aggravating ulcers. It is a frequent cause of automobile and other accidents; thus, when angry, we should never attempt to drive or to do anything that could be dangerous. Resentment causes women to be prone to household accidents. It increases the number of mistakes in decisions and in work of all kinds.

We can raise our existence to a saner, more successful, happier, and holier level by accepting the irremediable as God's beneficent will for us. We thus render ourselves immune to the infection of our character and life. When we begin to think how awful someone is, we should logically pray for him. Grace is evidently needed by the party, judging from our condemnatory thoughts. Thus we shall turn a temptation to unkindness into a helpful act, and everyone will be the better for it.

6. "Love Your Enemies"

I say to you who are listening: Love your enemies, do good to those who hate you. Bless those who curse you, pray for those who calumniate you . . . and you shall be children of the Most High, for he is kind towards the ungrateful and evil. Be merciful, therefore, even as your Father is merciful (Lk. 6:27–36).
Bless those who persecute you; bless and do not curse. . . . To no

man render evil for evil. . . . If it be possible, as far a be at peace with all men. Do not avenge yourselves, give place to the wrath, for it is written: "Vengea I will repay, says the Lord." . . . But "If the enemy is him food; if he is thirsty, give him drink. For by so wilt heap coals of fire upon his head" (Rom. 12:14–

It is obvious that love of our enemies does not mean tl love their character faults and misdeeds. These we may we wish well to their persons. We must not wish evil to God wishes well to all; and we must adopt God's attitude enemies. This is the rational attitude. Like the physician, the patient's disease but not the patient, we must not b hate the person of our neighbor because of his spiritual must love him the more, in our desire that he be cured.

An anonymous writer, probably of the second centu that the early Christians fulfilled the beautiful but he Christ. "Christians," he says, "love all men; and all me them."[16]

Christ's command is antipodal to brutish Communisn attitude of man in his highest reaches of nobility, dis genuine Christians, is also enjoined by fundamental n; We must love our enemies since they are our fellow crea by our common Creator, who, by creating us social, inte; wish only good to our fellow members of society.

The second and still more cogent reason for loving ou is that Christ accentuates this law by declaring that al His representatives and that whatever we do to the least o brethren we do to Him.

Third, if man has a greater love than that he lay dov for his friend, it is the love of Christ who lived and die and our enemies. Says St. Augustine:

He came into the world and found all men his enemies. no friend. For his enemies he shed his blood. But by his changed his enemies. He destroyed the sins of his ene his blood; and by destroying their sins, from enemies them his friends.[17]

16 *Epistle to Diognetus* 5, 11; cf. 6, 6.
17 *Serm.* 57, 10, 11; *PL* 38, 383, 4.

If we would love God greatly, we must have a great love of our enemies; for love of enemies is one of the advanced expressions of love of God. Christ made love the whole of Christianity: love of God, expressed largely through love of neighbor. If Christ, who had so much to suffer from His enemies and who yet loved them to the very limits of generosity — if Christ is to be the model of our love, it is clear that love of enemies is a substantial part of high love of God. All the great lovers of Christ are notable for love of their enemies.

Love him whom the beloved loves. By the fact that we are bid to "Love the Lord, thy God" we are implicitly bid to love our enemies since He loves them. Hence, Christ makes no exception when He commands us, "Love thy neighbor as thyself." He includes the neighbor who is our enemy. St. John Chrysostom was deeply impressed by this universality of love and impressed it deeply on his flock:

> Do you object that you honored someone and he vilified you? that you aided him and he wishes to kill you? If you love him on account of Christ, all such treatment will make your love still greater. He who loves because of Christ does not explore his neighbor's pedigree, nor his race, nor his wealth, nor how much he will be loved in return, nor any such circumstances; but even if he is hated and slandered, or even killed, he perseveres in his love, having plenty of reason for his love in his love of Christ. Hence, looking to Christ, he remains fixed, firm, and unchangeable in his love.[20]

St. Augustine proposes love of enemies as a capital means of progressing in love:

> As love of God grows in you, perfecting you and bringing you back to the likeness of God, it extends even to enemies, in order that you may be like Him. . . . The more you progress in likeness to Him, the more you progress in love; and to that extent you begin to feel (sentire) God. And whom do you feel? Him who comes to you and Him to whom you return. For He never goes away from you; God withdraws from you when you withdraw from God.[21]

---

20 *In Matt.* hom. 61; *PG* 58, 588.
21 *Ennar. in Ps.* 99:5; *PL* 37, 1273.

Blessed Claude de la Colombière, during his third year of novitiate at Paray-le-Monial in 1674, meditates on the love of the Sacred Heart for His enemies during His agony in the garden, as on a model for his own love of enemies.

> I behold this Heart which is without bitterness, without harshness, full of real tenderness toward His enemies, such that no perfidy, no evil treatment can move Him to hate. Then, addressing Mary to ask her to obtain for me the grace to put myself in the same disposition, I will consider that her heart is in the same sentiment as her Son's is; that she is engulfed in sorrow, with no unbefitting emotion; that she does not lose her tranquility of mind in such a terrible situation; that she does not will any harm to the torturers of her Son; that, on the contrary, she loves them and offers Him for their salvation.[22]

A further reason for love of our enemies is given us by God in the threat that if we do not forgive them, He will not forgive us. This reason is sufficient in itself to suppress any vindictive emotion at the injury done us by others; for, God knows, we have plenty for which we hope He will forgive us. Chrysostom warns of the seriousness of this threat:

> That which God hates and abhors most of all is remembrance of the wrongs we have suffered; and that which wins greatest acceptance from him is the opposite virtue [love of enemies].[23]

The righteous indignation of God at those who will not forgive others is powerfully portrayed by Christ in the indignation of the king who forgave his servant a great unpayable debt, and heard that the same servant imprisoned a fellow servant of the king, who could not pay him a much smaller debt. Christ concludes His story: "So also My heavenly Father will do to you, if you do not each forgive your brothers from your hearts." This parable and its conclusion were an illustration of his answer to Peter's question:

> "Lord, how often shall my brother sin against me, and I forgive him? Up to seven times?" Jesus said to him: "I do not say to thee seven times, but seventy times seven" (Mt. 18:21–35).

The spontaneous inference of the Apostles from this direction was

---

22 *Oeuvres complètes*, Grenoble, 1901, Vol. 6, p. 47 f.
23 In Mt. 6:14–15; *PG* 57, 282.

"Lord, increase our faith" (Lk. 17:5). Only deep faith can make us so deeply reasonable.

"Our friend the enemy" does us a real service in the opportunity he affords us of loving Christ sincerely and generously in our love for him; for Christ's command is that we love our enemies as He loved His.

St. Francis de Sales goes still farther:

> I have such pleasure, I experience sweetness so delicious and so special in love of my enemies, that if God would forbid me to love them I would have difficulty in obeying.[24]

"Only the stupid person," according to St. John Chrysostom, "will say: he is not my friend."

Enmity is illogical. Because someone has injured me and thereby hurt himself by his sin, it hardly follows that I also should descend to his level of irrationality in hurting him and myself by my sin. I do not better myself by taking on an enemy's malice.

Finally, enmity is abnormal psychology. St. Paul is teaching mental hygiene when he tells us that we should not let the sun set on our enmity (cf. Eph. 4:26). Enmities are termites eating away our reason and happiness, as well as the happiness of others. The first thing gnawed by the worm born in the wood is the wood in which it is born. St. Paul also calls enmities "works of the flesh" (Gal. 5:20), that is, not works of the rational spirit, but perverse yielding to blind emotion.

7. We Love Ourselves As We Love Others

All wishing of good for others, because it is the wish of God that we do so, is also the obtaining of good for ourselves. In the trinity of our loves, the love of God essentially begets the love of neighbor in its perfect likeness, and exclusively from both proceeds the proper love of ourselves.

Life begins with the act of creative love, with the begetting love

---

24 P. Camus, *The Spirit of St. Francis de Sales,* I, sec. 32.

of parents. Active life begins with the love in our instincts; and, essentially, life of the highest type is the highest type of love. If God's purpose for each of us is to love others as ourselves, it must be that such love is our own natural and supernatural good, for the purpose of the infinitely good God can be only for the happiness and worth of His creature. Conversely, it is disintegration of character and destruction of happiness and spirituality — often leading to neuroticism — to deteriorate to the attitude of loving no one.

Love of others is a principal glory to God, and consequently a principal perfection of man. The paradox follows that the more completely a human being loves others, just so much does he love himself. And one's love of others beautifies his own life, even more than it beautifies the life of his neighbor. Love is the only thing that, the more you give of it, the more you have of it, and the less you give of it, the less you have of it. If we dispense the perfume of happiness, we are bound to be redolent of it ourselves. We don't so much give happiness as exchange it.

There were once five brothers to whom their dying father left his flourishing business. He also left a sealed will, promising a million dollars among them, which they did not know he possessed, on condition that no brother ever quarreled with or was unkind to any other brother, and second, that they should work as a company in which they shared equally. The will was to be opened and executed ten years later. Although at times it was very difficult, the brothers managed to settle their differences amicably; and because of their complete co-operation, they became near millionaires by the time the will was to be opened. The will read as follows: "My dear sons, you already have the million dollars, and much more, which I have promised you if you were kind, forbearing, and co-operative with one another. Continue ever to be so; and you will be rich on earth and far richer in heaven."

While unkindliness shrivels up our person, love of others as ourselves multiplies us so that everyone is an "other ego," and our love is, as it were, our soul dwelling in other lives, each of whom is "half of my soul."

Christian love of others gives us liberty of action, liberty of thought, and liberty of emotion. Hate and ill-will are essentially confining. You may have experienced the entrance into a group of a character who quickly develops aversions: "I can't stand that person." "That fellow gets on my nerves." "He's impossible." Little by little he backs more or less alone into a corner of dislike. It is a commonplace in sane psychiatry that the only way to cure one's own sick heart is to seek to cure other sick hearts.

Dislike and ill-will gradually limit our sphere of life, until we are shut up in ourselves, in a confined and neurotic state. Love opens the whole world to our access. We can deal freely with all characters when we love them. The whole class of functional insanities have as their common denominator exaggerated concentration on self and alienation from others. How wise was the Maker of human psychology to raise, in the Mystical Body, our natural need for intercommunion to the dignity of a godly act.

"'Twas her thinking of others made you think of her," sang Elizabeth Browning. Love makes us lovely. What kind of eyes are the loveliest? Blue? Brown? . . . Kind eyes! The loveliest voice is the kind voice. Lovelier than all other hands are hands, whatever their shape, which are kind. Plain appearing persons, on more intimate experience, seem to grow more and more pleasant to look at, in their more and more evident beauty of kindness; while beautiful persons become strangely more and more repulsive and ugly in more intimate experience of their ugly unkindness. A beautiful face without kindness is an unlighted lamp. Children think their parents most beautiful if they are kind; as the Chinese proverb says, "There is only one beautiful woman in the world: every child's mother." The effort to be attractively interesting to others is what is known as "charm"; and charm is kindness in an effort to please others, as John M. Brown implies:

> Charm is the best of beauticians. It puts people at their ease, by putting *their* interests first and expressing, without selfconsciousness, a hospitable mind and heart. It is a soft and cushioning quality, which conquers by its graciousness. It prevents animation from being shrill, protects sweetness from cloying, and takes the malice out of curiosity.[25]

---

[25] In *Vogue*, Nov. 15, 1956.

Not only abstractly, but concretely, love is beauty. The fragrant aura of kindness makes us far more pleasant than the rarest essences of Araby. This embellishing cosmetic, this graceful jewelry, is within the means of all; but we ourselves must make it. Nothing else renders us so lovable to God and man as that we love others. On the other hand, as St. Paul instructs Titus (3:3), there is nothing that makes us so hateful as hate; in it we have clothed ourselves in the loathsome form of the demon.

8. *"Love Sincere Refines Upon the Taste"* (Colley Cibber)

Politeness as pure ceremonial is inane. An action is impolite only because it is unkind; and it is unkind because it is unsocial. Politeness is delicacy of understanding and practice of love of neighbor. That is what Emerson means when he teaches that "good manners are made up of petty sacrifices" to the sensibilities of our associates. Politeness is not supercilious criticism of others' manners. In fact, the test of good manners is to put up pleasantly with bad manners. Kindness, like politeness, is an expression of esteem and consideration for the person with whom we are dealing. We all desire esteem, since we interpret it as a form of love.

Will our action or our speech appear perfectly kind to our associates? Then it is perfectly polite. The so-called conventionalities of politeness are all developed with a view of sparing the feelings of others and of positively pleasing them. If a conventionality is not founded on kindness, it is meaningless artificiality, as devoid of content as a superstitious practice.

Cardinal Newman described politeness as kindness in social intercourse:

> The true gentlemen carefully avoids whatever may cause a jar or jolt in the minds of those with whom he is cast — all clashing of opinion, or collision of feeling, all restraint, or suspicion, or gloom, or resentment. His great concern is to make everyone feel

at their ease and at home. He has his eyes on all his company. He is tender toward the bashful, gentle toward the distant, and merciful toward the absurd. He can recollect to whom he is speaking; he guards against unreasonable allusions or topics which may irritate. . . .[26]

Whatever may be the human personality of our associates in their fusion through grace with the personality of Christ in the Mystical Body they are divine nobility, as far above the sublimest king or queen as the divine is above the human. They are courtly princes and princesses of the everlasting kingdom of God, deserving the most exquisite courtesy and most thoughtful graciousness. Impoliteness in, or toward, a member of the Mystical Body is the grossest of indecorum. Not without a basis in fact, the child prayed: "O Lord, make all the bad people good, and make all the good people nice."

Christian love is the perfecting of our mental judgment. *Ubi caritas, ibi claritas* — where there is love, there is clear thinking, whereas selfishness, the neutralizer of love, makes us blind, stupid, ignorant, imprudent, and unsuccessful. To live reasonably, we must love others and live for others. Self-seeking is always unreasonable and belittles us because of the errors which it brings us to commit in judgment and in practice. "Let this mind be in you, which was also in Christ Jesus," the kindly mind. The mind is, in great part, both the indication and the constitution of character. "As a man thinketh in his heart, so is he."

St. Paul describes in detail this principal theological virtue, which, by its nature, is eternal (1 Cor. 13). It gives the mind the invincibility of patience with injury to ourselves, and sympathy for the sorrow of others. It frees the mind from irrational jealousy; for, if we love God in fraternal love, we love to see Him better honored and more generously served in others than in ourselves. Such charity "rejoices not in wickedness," as those do who take satisfaction in seeing others do wrong, because thereby they themselves seem superior. This subtle joy in evil of others is love of self in preference to God, by which we stupidly think to appear to better advantage. For the same reason charity is not "puffed up" in its own excellence, but wishes that God be served even better by others

---

[26] *Idea of a University*, Pickering, London, ed. 3, p. 204.

than by ourselves. "Charity dealeth not perversely," for it is perversity to seek only self, and not primarily God, in our relations with our neighbor.

Let our mind, too, have the real broad-mindedness of Christ, making allowances for the shortcomings of others, not reacting violently to injuries, pitying others' woes.

> O God, that we could see a little clearer
> Or judge less harshly when we cannot see.
> O God, that we might draw a little nearer
> To one another. We'd be nearer thee. (*Anonymous*)

"Putting on Christ" means we put on the mind of Christ, not merely in kindness like His, but by partaking through grace of the individual mind and thought of Christ who thinks kindly of my neighbor through me.

True understanding of people must be light from the fire of love for them. Be kind, and you will find that what you thought to be deliberate unkindness in others is merely their lack of knowing how to be kind. Ask almost anyone: "Do you wish to be kind?" "Of course!" would be the answer. We all want to be kind. At our worst, we are thoughtless; or still oftener, we are mistaken in our reactions. What the unkind need is an atmosphere of kindness and the stimulus of its example. They are like children, grown up in the slums, who would like to be polite, but don't know how, or do not realize the impropriety of their actions and speech. By being kind, we effectively educate others in the ways of being kind; and they invariably correspond handsomely to our acceptable instruction.

> Be noble; and the nobleness that lies in other men
>   Sleeping, but never dead,
> Will rise in majesty to meet thine own. (Lowell — Sonnet IV)

9. Supernatural Influence

"He is truly great who has a great charity."[27] The supernatural is built upon the natural, and normally Christ in us has His super-

---

[27] *Imitation of Christ*, 1:3.

natural influence through our natural influence on others.

Invariably, "touchy" persons are the most inconsiderate of the feelings of others. Those who parade their deftness of wit in humiliating and poking fun at their slower minded associates react violently if anyone dare do the same to them. Hypersensitiveness runs exactly parallel with unwillingness to show due acknowledgment to others. How inconsiderate am I of others? I need but ascertain how considerate I am of myself. Selfishness and offense of others are so closely bound together, we cannot affect one without affecting the other. This should give us matter for serious thought, since we know that kindness is the invariable requisite for doing good to others.

Adler, the psychiatrist, has based his cure for the ills that the human mind is heir to on the fundamental principle that all man's seekings and instincts are variations of "the will to power over others." But he has exaggerated this truly powerful driving force. The greatest of all conquests, whatever should be said of Adler's theory, is influence over our fellow men. Force may enslave man's body, but it cannot subjugate his will; it cannot win his heart; and a subjugated body, in which dwells a rebellious will and heart, is by no means the conquest of a human being. Even though we silence his intellect by reasoning, even though we talk him dumb, without the agreement of his will, our conquest is a sham. "A man, convinced against his will, is of the same opinion still." How often a deaf ear has been turned to reason, when kindness would have gained a complete capitulation of the impregnable citadel of the heart. Christ, the fashioner of human psychology, in His own technique and approach to His mission of salvation, taught with infinite knowledge of the creature of His hands that kindness is the weapon to subdue the wayward human heart and headstrong mind. "It is difficult to realize," says Cicero, "how greatly men's minds are conciliated by a kind manner and gentle speech."[28]

We shall be able to work miraculous cures of human suffering, if, like St. Francis de Sales, we make kindness the first emergency dressing of the wounds we strive to heal. Kindness soothingly sterilizes the infection of bitterness, pride, selfishness, discouragement, while harshness causes the infection to penetrate more deeply, to spread

---

28 *De officiis,* 2, 15, 52.

more widely, and to generate a delirium of emotion. One need not be spiritual to see, with Victor Hugo, that "if you want to make men better, make them happier."

> To many a man, his only miracle,
> His one divine vision, his one remembered dream

is human kindness, says the poet Bridges; while Edna St. Vincent Millay sings:

> Many a man is making friends with death,
> Even as I speak, for lack of love alone.

Our eager instinct to find ourselves in others, to be in some way creators of their lives, can find fulfillment in the Mystical Body in almost any degree we wish. Our supernatural influence, the only influence of any value, is in proportion to our share in the Mystical Body and its activity; and that share is our sanctifying grace, which operates, not through our privilege of position, the acuteness of our abilities, or the worldly worth of our work, but to the extent that we participate in the Head and Life of the Mystical Body.

Earthly influence is disappointing, either in its meagerness or in its evanescence, and nearly always in both. Supernatural influence is the eternal act of God affecting the supernatural life of others, which becomes our influence through grace. When we are supernaturally kind, we allow Christ in us to influence His and our brethren, and His action becomes our own; and when we influence the members of the Mystical Body, we influence Christ and cause Him to grow in them.

10.   Exchange of Souls

When we in grace carry in ourselves the person of Christ, "who watched and wept and prayed and felt for all," how fittingly we sympathize with the sorrows and joys of others; and when we see Christ in others, how fitting it is that they receive our sympathy. Our sympathy, or "feeling with others," must be based on the worth of those with whom we sympathize; and the worth in others is Christ.

III. THE PRACTICE OF FRATERNAL CHARITY

1. *"What Is It But Mine Own Praise When I Praise Thee?"* (Shakespeare, Sonnet 39)

In everyone there is something praiseworthy. There is hardly any perfection so small that appropriate, sincere praise of it will not be most acceptable; and by our expressed esteem we encourage a development of importance. Praise is a very practical exercise of zeal for God's glory in the increase of perfection of our neighbor.

How often we find that we have enabled a person to produce above his capacity by our heartening appreciation of his accomplishment. On the other hand, by our faultfinding, we may have depressed the productiveness of a human life far below its potentiality, inducing in it an inferiority complex. Through so easy an effort as praise and interest in others, we can accomplish in them most valuable and happy effects, which are truly ours, inasmuch as they would not have been done were it not for our encouragement. In order to add new power and will and enthusiasm by encouraging a discouraged person — a relative, friend, associate — one is often much more effective by adroit recognition and admiration of his past successes without referring to his present difficulties.

God's desire for acknowledgment from His intellectual creatures arises fundamentally from His infinite love of the truth; and He has given His human creature a mind with the purpose that the truth be acknowledged above and before all else, in its Fountainhead, in Himself. "All true love is founded on esteem." We, too, imitate our Creator in our desire that the truth, which we are, be acknowledged by the esteem of our fellow men; and thus we feel that we are in some way loved. Our instinct for love from others, although not identical with it, is closely interwoven with our instinct for esteem from them. The perversion of this extremely strong tendency, pride, is an extremely strong vice. The desire of esteem, on the other hand, is not incompatible with humility, which is merely the exact and complete adherence to the truth concerning ourselves.

How spontaneously human beings seek approval is evident in the behavior of children from their earliest days of babyhood. They differ from adults, not in the intensity of their desire of approbation, but in their lack of camouflage of this desire. Esteem is our strongest stimulus to growth in worth, and, consequently, in glory to God, who can be glorified by His creatures only as they rise to greater perfection and worth.

Since esteem from others is an essential vitamin for human emotion and life, we are under a proportionate obligation, and Christ in us desires us, to afford the same to others. To deprive them of esteem is proportionately to cause them intense suffering and frustration. It follows that one of the most practical and productive ways of loving others is to give them the happiness and encouragement of our expressed esteem. It can be safely said that praise, if it has only altruistic ends, can rarely be too strong or too frequent. Yet, such is our perverse reluctance to show admiration of others, as though our standing would be diminished by it, that when we think that we are praising others extravagantly, we probably are expressing their just degree of praise. When others praise us highly, we accept it as justly due, unless, of course, it is obviously cynical and false. G. K. Chesterton had the outstanding ability of giving skillful, encouraging praise:

> Even more attractive to most of us was his fashion of making us feel that we had contributed something very worthwhile. He would take something, that one had said, and develop it until it shone and glowed, not from its own worth, but from what he had made of it.[1]

2. *Criticism: "The Sin in Loving Virtue"* (Shakespeare, "Measure for Measure")

There is a perverse seeking of the appearance of importance instead of its reality, and this is seen especially in some forms of criticism.

---

[1] M. Ward, *G. K. Chesterton* (New York: Sheed and Ward, 1943), p. 204.

Bad criticism works unrealized devastation, both in the individual infected and in the society which he infects. In gossiping Rome, St. Ignatius was well aware of the demolition wreaked in the Church by ecclesiastical criticism. Sending a Jesuit to Flanders he warned him: "Do not speak unfavorably of Pope Paul IV!"

"But," objected the Father, "I cannot bring myself to approve of some of his measures."

"Well, then, talk of Pope Marcellus!" was Ignatius' rejoinder.

There is of course, a kind, constructive criticism, a perfecting of the Christ in others by helping them to overcome their faults. But, in the main, criticism is destructive, a sinister bent to find fault with others, by which the critic deviously and speciously enjoys a sense of importance, a fallacious feeling that he is praiseworthy in perceiving and indicating the failings of others. The exact opposite is true. Constructive criticism has, as its test, the desire to do good, to love others. Destructive criticism seeks to hurt others, to diminish or destroy their good names, generally as a shift to bolster up one's own esteem, or as a more or less hysterical escape from self-condemnation.

The critic himself, with all other people, admires the one who is very slow to criticize and very ready to praise others. Indirect praise is to be gained only by showing appreciation of others: "What is it but mine own praise when I praise thee?" (Shakespeare, Sonnet 39.) The cynical critic is a destroyer of society. He is often poor wine gone sour. While he does not please as wine, as vinegar he forces us to take notice of his acerbity. All are painfully aware of the presence of the sharp-tongued critic; and fortunate is the community in which the vinegary faultfinder does not sour a great deal of its sweetness. Peevish criticism is more likely to rise in us when we feel more acutely our inferiority or lack of success or notice.

The more acutely one feels an inferiority complex, the more he is tempted to compensate for it by narrating the evils of others, by gossiping. The more gossipers feel defeated in getting the esteem they desire, the more they seek to defeat the desire of others for esteem by wrecking their reputations. Talebearers similarly want to appear, before the one to whom they carry the tale, better than those whom they denounce. But, as in all neurotic procedures, the talebearer besmirches his own name in besmirching the name of others: "the

talebearer shall defile his own soul, and shall be hated by all; and
he that shall abide with him shall be hateful" (Ecclus. 21:31). We
should act as St. Augustine's mother, St. Monica, whom he praises
as one who often heard both sides of complaints, rancor, and resentment, and never carried it from one side to the other, while she
strove, as an angel of peace, to explain away resentment and to
mollify the feelings of the quarrelsome.

A notable increase in criticism frequently is a symptom of dis-
integrating character and mentality. A common phenomenon of a
genus of insanity is letter writing to all sorts of officials, high and low,
correcting them in their government. Here, we find that the good
done is often more severely censured than that which is evil; and
superior persons are deprecated more than inferior ones. "If I can
find fault with a superior person," the carper unconsciously reasons, "I will appear still more superior." He fools no one but
himself. Strange, isn't it, how clearly we see this in others, and how
little in ourselves?

Mentally privileged persons often nurse a sense of inferiority that
is far more acute than it is in the underprivileged. Neurotically
they resent some deficiency in their character, and this gives rise to
their faultfinding, a concealed protest, when we would expect them
to be cheerfully indulgent toward the defects of others. They are
often like the Assyrian Aman, who ate out his heart because, although he was highly honored by the king and populace, there was
one wretched Jewish prisoner who would not bow as he passed by.

One never paints his own character in such highlights as when he
portrays the character of another. We understand best of all in others
the vices in which we ourselves fail; and understanding them perfectly, we hate them more intensely in others. Hart analyzes this
"projection" thus:

> The personality avoids conflict (of conscience and offense) by
> "projecting" the offending complex on to some other person,
> where it can be efficiently rebuked, without the painful emotion
> which inevitably accompanies the recognition of deficiencies in
> ourselves.[2]

Undoubtedly, there is the possibility of understanding people bet-

---

[2] *Psychology of Insanity,* Cambridge U. Press, 1922, p. 120.

ter by realizing that they have our desires, feelings, emotions, ambitions, and noble purposes; but we must beware of any self-justification for our faults because others have them. People who are notably guilty of a certain failing are proverbially intolerant of that failing in others. Who blames a proud person more violently than another proud person? To a thief, no one could be anything but a thief, at least in heart. For the unchaste person, it is utterly impossible that there are chaste persons. The upstart is the most loudly contemptuous of the more recent upstart.

3. *Defamation*

To speak of another's sin, whether truly or mendaciously, can easily be a far greater sin than to commit the sin oneself. A young man was convicted of a crime and served a year in the penitentiary. Really repentant, he married in a town where he was unknown, and became a person of great good influence in his community. After thirty years of valuable life, a man in the town discovered that he had been a convict and published the fact, completely destroying his victim's name and influence. Far more criminal and ignominious was the detractor's sin than if he himself had committed the crime and served the sentence as a convict.

Would that this outrageous pharisaical sin of defamation by telling the truth were not so common among those who believe themselves to be the Lord's nobility! Would, at least, that they were aware of the mortal injury inflicted on their own souls! Would that, before they give their account to God, they realized the appalling load of obligatory restitution burdening their conscience!

Calumny, or slander, is a lie by which we injure the good name of another. To the grave injury of defamation it adds a depraved lie. But it is hard to say whether this or detraction is the greater sin. Slander is worse inasmuch as it is also a lie; but detraction can easily be much worse than slander in the injury done, because there is no possibility of disproving the fact told and of repairing the injury. "The greater the truth, the greater the libel."

In defamation there is a whole gang of vices. Its leader is the sin against love of neighbor, which is very often and very easily grievous, because it hurts him in the worst possible way, in his reputation, on which practically all the phases of his life depend. It causes him poignant pain.

> The stroke of a whip maketh a blue mark:
> but the stroke of the tongue will break the bones.
> Many have fallen by the edge of the sword,
> but not so many as have perished by their own tongue. . . .
> The death thereof is a most evil death:
> and hell is preferable to it (Ecclus 28:21–25).

The greatness of the sin of defamation is measured by the greatness of the injury it does to another. As Christians, we must realize the extreme intensification of this injury, inasmuch as it is done to Christ Himself. Christ with His grace must leave the soul of the defamer who realizes what he is doing, for destruction of reputation is a mortal sin.

God made man social, and for social existence and perfection a good name is essential. Hence, ethics rightly concludes that God, by giving man such a nature, intended him to have the right to a good name, and intended others to have the obligation not to injure it, even by telling the truth, except when a greater good demands it.

Reputation is surpassingly valuable in man's social life, business life, family life, and spiritual life. An injury to it can be a manifold injury, or even a complete paralysis of all functions that are human. Loss of goods cannot be compared with loss of reputation. If our purse or material goods are stolen, we can get others; but the theft of our reputation robs us both of our greatest treasure and of our ability to restore it.

The esteem of others and their resulting confidence in us give us a reassuring confidence in ourselves and an energetic enthusiasm in our work. We are happy in that love which is indicated in the esteem of our associates. "A good name is better than precious ointments" (Eccles. 7:2) in making us agreeable to others. A good reputation certainly opens hearts and souls to our influence as nothing else does. When a good reputation goes ahead of us, it prepares the field of our activity to an optimum condition and widens it to its utmost. If a precursor has blackened our name, on our arrival we find all doors firmly shut to us as to the pest. The wreckage of human endeavor and human influence is especially calamitous when the reputation is that of a person who has authority over others, such as a parent, a teacher, an official, a priest, or other leader. Especially in them, as Livy maintains, "Injury done to good name and character is greater than can be estimated."[3]

"Who hath not owned the magic of a name?"[4] Destroy that name, and we destroy the magic which makes wonderful things possible. Destroy esteem, and you dig a deep, wide moat between the person and all those who thereby lose their esteem for him. We very rightly take care of our good name, for it is more important than money in the business of living. "Take care of a good name: for this shall continue with thee, more lasting than a thousand treasures precious and great" (Ecclus. 41:15).

How sensitive men are to the least rumpling of the fine cloth of their good name! How furious they are inclined to become, if one makes a tear in it! God gave man this instinctive, inevitable desire of esteem, so that he would make himself worthy of it by perfecting himself in the eyes of God and of his fellows. Rob a man of his desire of esteem, cut off his opportunity to win it, and you have robbed him of his power to live a human life.

No one, whatever he may fondly believe his character to be, tough or tender, cynic or ascetic, is without vivid appreciation of human esteem. No one can put off his human nature, from which this high evaluation of a good name arises.

To destroy so precious a treasure as reputation is a villainous crime. It is beyond all infamy, lightly and out of mere desire to make conversation, to assert the unfounded gossip that comes into our tickled ears, and the unfounded ideas that come into our irresponsible minds, against the name of another. It is while a person is idle that the tongue works hardest in its demolition of valuable reputations.

---

[3] *Annals*, 3, 72.
[4] Campbell, *The Pleasures of Hope.*

When we have painstakingly put away furs or fine woolens in the spring, and go to take them out for the coming of winter, how keenly disappointed we are, in expectation of their use, when we find that moths have ravaged them. But incalculably greater is our neighbor's chagrin when he wishes to use a carefully preserved reputation and finds that we have gnawed gaping holes in it.

Scandals are decomposing corpses; they should be buried as infectious. Perhaps the second in power of defamation's gang of vices is its infection of others. Besides the general effect of scandal in making those ready to do wrong who hear that others do wrong, desire is excited to hear what it is a sin to wish to hear, contrary to the Wise Man's inspired instruction: "Hedge in thy ears with thorns, hear not a wicked tongue" (Ecclus. 28:28) and to the warning of Proverbs: "Have nothing to do with detractors" (*ibid.* 24:21). Moreover, the hearer will probably multiply the defamation, as well as embroider it. Those most eager to know secrets are the ones most eager to destroy their secrecy by incontinently publicizing them. Spendthrifts long for money, not to keep it, but to squander it. Detractors long for secrets, not to keep them, but to broadcast them.

As we stand before God, surely we have enough in our own sins to occupy our attention and righteous indignation, especially as God is the one who taught us to pray for forgiveness to the extent that we forgive others. Surely, too, our personal sins are a sufficiently crushing burden, without taking upon us the burdens of dozens, and even of hundreds, of detractors who sprout from our spore!

Very few persons are ready to counterfeit money, but many will feloniously pass on what they know to be counterfeit. Many, who are not ready to manufacture lying defamation, do not scruple to circulate what they well know is probably a lie, or surely will become one.

> Hast thou heard a word against thy neighbor?
> Let it die there, . . . trusting
> it will not burst thee (Ecclus 19:10).

The third deadly member of defamation's gang is its destruction of peace in the community. "The whisperer . . . hath troubled many that were at peace" (*ibid.* 28:15). Our maligning of others gives rise to intense bitterness and dissension, revenge of any and all sorts, loss of happiness here, and often hereafter. "He that repeateth (a transgression) separateth friends" (Prov. 17:9). St. Basil directed that not only the religious who spoke of the faults of others should be isolated from the community in confinement, but also the one who listened to the detractor; for, if one had not willingly listened, the other would not have recounted his scandalous story.

"The words of a talebearer . . . reach to the innermost parts of the belly [emotions]" (*ibid.* 26:22). It is because of the frustration of our powerful instinct and need for esteem that we are so incensed at gossip about us. "When the wood faileth, the fire shall go out; and when the talebearer is taken away, contention shall cease" (*ibid.* 26:20).

Among defamation's vices, there is always one that destroys or seriously injures the rash defamer himself. We would be fiercely indignant were someone to call us a thief. Defamation makes us the vilest of thieves; for the gossiping detractor steals a person's most valuable possession, his good name, usually in the dark, without gaining thereby, and merely to steal.

Instead of being fully engrossed in our own business, many of us dribble away our precious time, and that of others, in vacuous chatting which cannot sustain itself on the news of the day; and so we assault the good name of others.

> Being idle, they learn to go about from house to house, and are not only idle, but gossipers as well and busybodies, mentioning things they ought not (1 Tim. 5:13).

Defamation is not only murderous to the reputation of others; it is suicidal to our own. Not only are detractors "hateful to God" (Rom. 1:30), they are also "the abomination of men" (Prov. 24:9). From our experience, we can know that others, listening to our disgusting defamation, say to themselves: "I suppose that this defamer speaks about me in the same way when I am absent." A really noble person is liable to think in his heart: "Well, that's the end of my friendship with this detractor!" Whatever the guilt of the defamed may be, incriminating others, we certainly incriminate ourselves, of crime often worse than that of which we speak.

Stupidity is no name for the absurd thought that we make ourselves agreeable to others by talebearing, gossip, backbiting, and

"cutting of men's throats by whisperings."[5] They may be eagerly
interested in what we say, they may admire the manner of our
narration, but in their hidden judgment they despise us. Everyone
except the naïve defamer sees the abnormality of mind which thinks
to appear better by making others appear worse. Defamation is not
only anti-Christian; it is also irrational. We need but have the use
of reason to see its wretchedness. The pagan Plautus feels this way
about it:

> You tittle-tattlers, and you who listen to their slanderous tales,
> If I had my way, you should all be hanged,
> The former by your tongues, the latter by your ears.[6]

Apart from the fact that it is defamatory, defamation usually
involves a secret. A neighbor's secret, whether of person, family, or
business, must be regarded as sacred, so that we may not seek to
learn it or to make it known. The reason is that the good of society,
and consequently the intention of God, enjoins that persons or
groups should have their secrets inviolate. A secret is a good of the
soul, a right given by nature and by nature's Creator. We must not
deprive our neighbor of this good and right, unless the good of
society demands that we make it known to the proper persons, but
only to them.

The degree of injury to fraternal charity in betrayal of a secret
depends on the importance of the secret, which may be natural, that
is, of its very nature a secret, for instance illegitimacy of birth, or a
criminal record; or it may be a promised secret, or a secret of trust,
arising from an implicit contract. This contract is supposed between
clients and professional persons, such as physicians, lawyers, priests,
or counselors. Teachers, nurses, social workers, and domestic servants
frequently injure society by needlessly manifesting the secrets of
the persons with whom they deal.

The inviolability of the secret in letters is a great good to society,
and it is immoral to read them, opened or unopened. The only
reason that can justify newspaper publication of secrets is the good
of society. For some "yellow journals" the mere fact that something
is a secret is a reason for publishing it. The obligation to keep secrets

---

[5] Ben Jonson, *Sejanus*, 1, 1.
[6] *Persa*, 3, 1.

is, in general, one of fraternal charity; but if foreseen injury to a person is the result of needless revelation of a secret, there is an added obligation of justice to repair the injury.

4. *"If You Would Be Perfect" Speak No Ill of Others*

Meticulous carefulness in the way in which we speak of others' defects is one of the practical tests by which we show whether we understand perfection of living and are earnest in our efforts to attain it. This concern is characteristic of St. Ignatius of Loyola; he kept extreme silence about the defects of those in the house with him and of those outside, speaking of them only to those who were able to remedy them. If it were sufficient that only one person knew the fault in order to correct it, he took care not to tell two. Superiors under him had to take his severe reprehension for weakening the confidence of their subjects by making known their faults needlessly. A superior should be a parent who sedulously hides the faults of the children from outsiders.

Let everyone feel assured that his precious reputation will not suffer in your keeping, either in great or in small matters. If they are sure that their good name will rather be increased when you have anything to say about them, they will be disposed in the very best way to receive your influence. Otherwise, you can do nothing with them; for they will hold that you are inimical to them, and not without reason.

While it is usually more than doubtful that blunt public denouncement of the detractor is advisable, every hearer, and especially a superior, should examine his conscience: "Could I have efficiently and adroitly stopped the detraction? Was I in any way the cause or encouragement of the sin, for instance, by asking questions or showing interest?" It is said of St. Augustine that he reminded his guests by a Latin couplet painted on the dining-room wall that he did not want any defamation at his table:

> Who gnaws good name with biting jest
> Is at this board unwelcome guest.

If we rob a person of the capital on which he lives, if we purposely burn down his business building with all its stock, obviously we are bound before God to labor all our lives to reimburse him. Much more are we bound in justice and in charity to labor tirelessly and endlessly to restore his reputation which we have inconscionably destroyed, and on which he much more truly depends for life. If the injury which we do to a person's reputation be grave, as it very easily can be, the obligation of restitution is grave. What an appalling load of obligation to carry! The gravity of injury by detraction, and of the obligation to repair the injury, depends on:

1. The nature of the injury done.
2. The person defamed: a parent? a spouse? a merchant? physician? judge? superior? teacher? priest?
3. The number of persons by whom the evil will be heard.

We must, therefore, restore the defamed person's reputation, in the minds of all those to whom we have repeated the detraction, and also in all the minds to whom our hearers have repeated the detraction. More easily will you collect all the flying seeds of a dandelion, and all the seeds that have sprouted from those seeds!

An especially virulent gossip of Rome, who believed herself to be quite spiritual, was plucking a chicken before her house door, in a pan under a cloth because of a brisk wind that was blowing. Philip Neri, the saintly prankster, was passing that way and stopped to greet her. Just as a gust of wind struck them, he jerked the cloth from over the pan, and hundreds of feathers went flying through the city. Before the housewife could protest, he told her: "You'll have to gather those feathers." Rather piqued, she retorted: "That would be a fine job!" Making his point, he drove home his lesson: "It's easier to gather those feathers than to undo the effects of your flying gossip."

If people were to receive ten dollars every time they speak kindly of others, and if they had to give five dollars every time they speak unkindly of another, many would be thousands of dollars in debt. In such an arrangement, would I be in the red?

5. *"Judge Not!"*

We must not believe that we are inculpable in thinking ill of others merely because we do not speak ill of them to anyone. We are speaking ill of them to ourselves. We must protect everyone's good name, not only in conversation with others, but also in mental conversation with ourselves. The science of ethics, as well as the still more cogent theology of Christ, demands that we do not allow rash judgments of others to find reception in our mind. Such judgments are rash in more than one way.

First, we have no right to take upon ourselves the juridical powers of God. We ought to hear God speaking to us through Job (13:8): "Do you endeavor to judge for God?" and through Jeremias (29:23): "I am the judge and the witness, saith the Lord." This all the more, since Christ says to us, as He said to the Pharisees: "Let him that is without sin cast the first stone" (Jn. 8:3–11).

Second, in rash judgment we are a criminal who would presume to be a judge condemning his fellow criminals, "a juryman guiltier than the one he tries."[7] When we catch ourselves in such shameless effrontery before God and heaven, it is highly advisable to squelch such thoughts with the admonition: Mind your own business! St. Paul energetically brings this home to us:

> Wherefore, thou art inexcusable, O man, whoever thou art who judgest. For wherein thou judgest another, thou dost condemn thyself. For thou who judgest dost the same things. . . . Dost thou think, O man who judgest those who do such things and dost the same thyself, that thou wilt escape the judgment of God? (Rom. 2:1 ff.)

Third, the good of human nature, intended by its Creator, demands that we avoid this fouling up of human relations and of our mind. Love of neighbor involves wishing him well as the basis of doing him good, and rash judgment is anything but that.

Fourth, rash judgment is roundly condemned for its irrationality

---

[7] Shakespeare, *Measure for Measure*, 2, 2, 76.

by Christ, who reserves to His omniscience all judgment of men. "Do not judge, and you shall not be judged; do not condemn, and you shall not be condemned" (Lk. 6:37). St. Matthew (7:1–3) records our Lord's teaching on this matter: "Do not judge, that you may not be judged. For with what judgment you judge, you shall be judged." In other words, we have our Lord's promise that, if we are merciful in our thoughts of others, He will be merciful in His judgment of us.

The Apostles evidently found among early Christians, as we find today, ample reason for strongly emphasizing this doctrine of their Master, for they dwell on it frequently and seriously. For instance, St. Paul (Rom. 14:4, 10, 11, 13) warns the Christians of Rome:

> Who art thou to judge another's (God's) servant? To his own lord he stands or falls . . . why dost thou judge thy brother? . . . For we shall all stand at the judgment-seat of God. . . . Therefore let us no longer judge one another.

The Apostle gives the same lesson to the Christians of Corinth (1 Cor. 4:5):

> Pass no judgment before the time, until the Lord comes, who will both bring to light the things hidden in darkness and make manifest the counsel of hearts. . . .

St. John also reminds his Christians not to usurp Christ's prerogative of Judge: "God has given all judgment to the Son" (Jn. 5:22). St. James gives the same inspired warning (4:11–13):

> Brethren, do not speak against one another. He who speaks against a brother, or judges his brother, speaks against the law and judges the law. But if thou judgest the law, thou art not a doer of the law, but a judge. There is one Lawgiver and Judge. . . . But thou who judgest thy neighbor, who art thou?
> Behold the judge is standing at the gate (*ibid.* 5:9).

Fifth, no one can do personal right or wrong unless and inasmuch as he knows that he is doing so. We cannot see the interior of a person's mind and will, on which his morality and immorality depend, even though we perfectly evaluate the exterior action. It is truly remarkable how we interiorly consider the evil in our wrong action to be much less than those who perceive the act exteriorly; and one is guilty in conscience only inasmuch as he considers himself to be guilty. Our judgment of others, then, is usually rash because it is passed without knowledge of a crucial fact of the case, namely, the conscience of the one we judge. "Judge not by appearances, but give just judgment" (Jn. 7:24) is our Lord's appropriate warning.

Full knowledge of the degree of immorality of an act as well as full freedom of choice is necessary in order that an act be formally evil. We cannot know the degree of free choice operative in an immoral action; and also for this reason we had better refrain from judging another's guilt.

The freedom of choice of an immoral act can be diminished, or even nullified, by invincible ignorance of its immorality, and by quite a number of factors influencing the will. Strong instincts or tendencies, sometimes called "passions," may exert any degree of suppression of free choice. Such passions as anger, lust, jealousy, melancholy, forestall reason or blind it, to some extent or totally. Thus the intellect is not correctly informed in its guidance of the will; and the will is weakened or overcome. The brother who killed his brother at the termination of a very angry quarrel that developed over a mere thirty cents certainly was not fully guilty of fratricide. How guilty he was, if at all, who but God knows? Fear or surprise may also lessen free choice. "Brethren, if a person is caught doing something wrong, you who are spiritual instruct such a one in a spirit of meekness, considering thyself, lest thou also be tempted" (Gal. 6:1). All things considered, we have no right to judge the morality of another's act "until all the facts are in," which well may not be in this life.

Even our Lord was the victim of rash judgment (Lk. 7:39). Simon the Pharisee was indignant at His kindness to a sinner: "This man, were he a prophet, would surely know who and what manner of woman this is who is touching him, for she is a sinner." Because Anna (1 Kings 1), in her grief, prayed to God in her heart and moved only her lips without praying aloud, as was the custom, Heli, the high priest, rudely told her that she was drunk and to get out of the temple until she was sober. Not so God, who heard her prayer.

6. The Social Psychology of Christ

When we show some knowledge of the laudable facts in the lives of others, we compliment them for we thus show that their lives and persons are worth knowing and remembering: their business, their families, their hobbies, and other interests. We fail as conversationalists by talking too much about ourselves and not enough about our listeners, which amounts to saying that we consider ourselves and our interests of more importance than theirs. Besides, when we talk about ourselves, we learn nothing; when we talk about the interests of others, we, with time, learn a great deal. A good listener honors the speaker; and all of us find an interested hearer to be as agreeable as a perfect fit in shoes.

God shows His infinite interest in each of us, be we as lowly as an abandoned babe on a China highway. He tells us that He knows us personally, that He thinks of us individually, and that He is always aware of us and of our minute personality: "Fear not, for I have redeemed thee and called thee by name: thou art mine" (Isa. 43:1). There is hardly a more pleasant word in the language than one's own name, spoken with recognition of our personality. Hence, we should make a pronounced effort to remember the names of acquaintances and to give them the gratification of feeling that they are sufficiently important for us to remember their names.

Our admiration of the activities and occupations of others renders them happy in our appreciation of them. The Christ indwelling in us, with whom we should think, is extremely interested in the activity of our fellows. Generally we should imply that our hearers are in a successful position, socially, economically, domestically, or otherwise, and that they are, at least, on a level with us. The asking of favors, which others are glad to give, also augments their sense of importance. By seeking to be of service judiciously and by showing them graceful attentions, we give them pleasure for the same reason. "Can I be of service to you?" is a most agreeable question to hear. By appropriately asking the opinion of others, we show esteem for their judgment and experience. Imitation, when possible, is also great praise.

Deference to another in speech and action gratifies him and asserts his importance to us; and certainly deference is due to the Christ whom he represents, or who dwells in him through grace. Deference restrains our offensive assertion of self-importance, so that we do not "crowd" others, either in speech, movement, arrangement, or place. We give all ample room to speak, to appear, and to act, with facility and dignity. For this reason, judicious allowance of self-assertion, self-direction, and initiative to others is kindness that is Godlike and wise.

One of the reasons why liberty is prized, even above life, is that it affords us expression of our own importance. Proper obedience does not imply a suppression of initiative. It is real kindness, and cleverness besides, to let those under you think that the idea which they follow is their own. How often opposition is generated by the mere fact that action is totally dictated.

Charity will lead us to give others opportunity to shine, say, by assigning a task of activity, so adapted to the doer, so definite, and with such adequate means, that he feels confident of success and finds himself on a stage, perfectly set to display his ability and worth to the full. No other treatment of Christ is thinkable.

All human contacts should be made in a friendly spirit. We should have a kindly feeling toward all, and show it with a smile, no matter what the nature of our social, domestic, or business contact may be. This is Christ's demand of us: love all! A smile assures us of a fair consideration and of a square deal. A smile tells us that, even though we do not obtain what we desire, at least there is no prejudice against us. A long face, a serious look, leaves us in doubt as to whether the person is not prejudiced against us. When you have something disagreeable to say, say it with benevolence. Is there any other ordinary way of addressing Christ than with a benevolent smile? When we must correct — and many correct much too often for kindness, and even for efficiency — we should show our respect for the person corrected. In all correction or blame of another, it is essential to Christ's action in us that we manifest kindly dispositions toward Him in the corrected person, and that we make it clear that we are solely concerned with his good, and not with perverse satisfaction in correcting or blaming others. If we are motivated only by kindness, we shall give the corrected one an opportunity to "save face"; for it is generally vicious to so reprehend another that he is forced into total "loss of face."

When we disagree with another — in general we disagree much too often, both for the good of kindness and even for truth — we should, as a matter of course, first express that in which we agree with him: "I see we agree in some essentials; we can probably come to more or less complete agreement." Above all, we should avoid such uncouth expressions as: "No! you're wrong."

Blunt contradictions, if frequent, bespeak lack of culture, to say nothing of the lack of reverence for the Christ in others. Consequently, it is usually advisable to delay an outright rejection of another's proposal. We ask for time to think it over, even though we are sure we must reject it. Some have so tactful and kindly a way of refusing us that their refusal is second in pleasantness only to the granting of our desire. Some know how to disagree with us so painlessly that for some time we are not fully aware that they do not agree with us. Instead of contradicting, we can sometimes rephrase another's incorrect assertion or proposal, so that the one making it will allow it to stand as his own: "I agree with you that . . . ," or like Anthony in Shakespeare's *Julius Caesar:* "I tell you that which you yourselves do know."

This is kindness directly opposite to the perverse tendency to twist another's words into a sense that is obviously false or mean. Hence, we should imply that a person is acting under correct and noble motives. In this manner, we shall lead him so to act, if in fact he has not been. Thus, in seeking cheerfulness in his patient, the physician says at the least opportunity: "It's a pleasure to care for one so cheerful as you"; or if he wishes more exactness in carrying out his prescriptions, he praises the patient's co-operation in following the diet or in taking medicine regularly as directed. The businessman insists tactfully on the payment of bills by his praise: "It is very satisfactory to extend credit to persons like you, who are so prompt in settling their accounts." The mother tells her boy, on the occasion of a perhaps too rare gracious act toward his sister:

"You make me so happy, Johnny, when I see how considerate you are of your sister." In announcing his political candidate, the manager praises the acumen of his hearers: "Here is the upright, wise, and capable mayor that your civic intelligence and pride has been looking for."

7. To Be Right Is Not Always to Be Perfect

Incalculable is the demolition of human happiness and peace of mind, irremediable is the damage of human values in every way, enormous is the loss and hindrance of grace effected by conflicts of mere opinions which are often of little or no consequence to the ones holding them.

Even though we know that another's expressed opinion is wrong, we are still worse by insisting on our right opinion, with the clear knowledge that the only result of such insistence will be harmful to the feelings of another. Why should we do that which has only an evil effect? Some seem to think that to have "the courage of one's convictions" means to try to force them on others, with little further concern, in many cases, about living up to them. To assert one's precious ideas in pointed contradiction to others is rarely courage, but an emotional attitude like that of one who will fight for his religion, but will not practice it properly.

To be right is not always to be perfect; and to be perfect is not necessarily to manifest oneself as perfect. The Christ who would express Himself in us is the Christ who was ready to appear wrong when He was misrepresented to Pilate as a disturber of the peace while He was the Prince of Peace. At times, to be wrong and to admit it simply is a greater perfection than to be right. In many cases, it is a far greater perfection of character, and even of intellect, to yield to another who is wrong and to yield to his misjudgment than to reject his mistaken judgment to his discomfiture and humiliation.

That sage of modern times, G. K. Chesterton, amiably teaches:

There is no better test of a man's ultimate chivalry and integrity, than how he behaves when he is wrong; and Johnson behaved very well. He understood, what so many faultlessly polite people do not understand, that a stiff apology is a second insult. He understood that the injured party does not want to be compensated because he has been wronged; he wants to be healed because he has been hurt. . . . He did not waste time in formally withdrawing this word with reservations and that word with explanations. Finding that he had given pain, he went out of his way to give pleasure. If he had not known what would irritate Boswell, he knew what would soothe him. It is this gigantic realism in Johnson's kindness, the directness of his emotionalism, when he is emotional, that gives him his hold upon generations of living men.[8]

Thousands of years more before Christ than there are years after Him, allowance was made in architecture and art for defective human vision; from which we can take the lesson that, if we are to build a perfect architecture of life, we must accommodate ourselves often to the defective opinions and actions of others. Egyptian obelisks of the thirtieth century before Christ are of remarkable refinement in design. Not only is their taper in proportion to their height and width, but the sides of their shafts are cut with a slight convexity, or "entasis," to compensate for the eye's perception of them as concave. We can well incorporate this asymmetry of the early Egyptians, or departure from geometrical correctness, into the work of art that is our living with others.

To allow others to remain in undisputed possession of their opinions in most cases where assertion of our true opinion would cause only sterile or destructive conflict is a sign of a nicely balanced sense of values. Such are the really tolerant persons. Dogmatism, in matters of little or no dependence on our assertion of them, is only the fault of childish minds. Dryden, in his description of an individual,

> Stiff in opinions,
> Always in the wrong,[9]

is close to a description of a general truth. Force is the destruction of liberty; and opinion, sometimes in the name of liberty of opinion, will not hesitate to use force to destroy that liberty. One

---

[8] *The Common Man* (New York: Sheed and Ward, 1950), pp. 120–121.
[9] *Absalom and Achitophel.*

should think that we would be more ready to put our opinion in our pocket, and leave it there, when its expression would result only in evil, since

> We praise at morning what we blame at night,
> But always think our last opinion right.[10]

Science, without charity, is barbarity. It is seemly, then, as the Church has more than once urged, to allow official ecclesiastical authority the exclusive right to call the adversaries of our opinions heretics. This un-Christian, unscientific faith in our personal infallibility as regards questions disputed among worthy teachers, "whose praise is heard in the Church," is plainly the vice of contention, discord, and quarrelsomeness.[11] "Some indeed preach Christ even out of envy and contentiousness" (Phil. 1:15). In the sight of those who are too ready to damn the Church for unreasonableness, "let us walk becomingly . . . not in strife and jealousy" (Rom. 13:13); for "the Lord hateth . . . him that soweth discord among brethren" (Prov. 6:19).

8. Love As World Government

Love of our neighbor, willing the peace of order for all men and nations, supposes a world federation with supreme authority over all nations, with adequate legislature, courts, and police force, just as we have cities under a state government and states under the Federal Government. It is clear from reason and from history that there can be no durable peace without "the existence of the law of love and of brotherhood, which embraces and holds all nations and peoples in a single family, with one Father who is in heaven." This objective of Pope Pius XI (1933) means that, as in a family, the stronger nations are to develop the weaker ones, instead of growing stronger by exploiting the weaker, who in desperation are ready to

---

[10] Pope, *Essay on Criticism*, II, 230.
[11] Cf. St. Thomas, 2–2, 38, 1.

resort to internecine war in order to escape from intolerable conditions forced upon them. Love of neighbor means collective family responsibility for the well-being of all nations. It requires that wealthier nations raise the level of living in poorer nations, by affording immigration into large unoccupied areas, by teaching them industrial know-how, and by affording reasonable access to the raw stuffs of commerce and to markets for products.

"There is no such thing as inevitable war," Bonar Law declared in the British Parliament, shortly before World War I. "If war comes, it will come from failure in human wisdom." War by governments must be changed to peace by peoples. "Peace," wisely observed Ramsay MacDonald (House of Commons, March 21, 1934), "depends on international cooperation; and peace is the only security." Thus alone there will be "liberty in tranquillity" as Cicero defines peace.[12]

Pope Pius XII (*Summi Pontificatus*) urged, for correct relations of peace between nations, the intrinsic right to liberty and security from aggression, equitable opportunities for commerce and material welfare, general disarmament, a Federal World-State with a World-Court, administration and sanction in order to settle international conflicts without war and in order to reconstruct international order according to the principles of brotherly love.

This form of United Nations is the right "Universal Governor" urged by Dante in his "Banquet." The Natural Law demands the "*Civitas Maxima*," the superstate (Marcus Aurelius). By nature, man forms "one world," one human family, requiring one government. The probability that this will not happen, because of the materialistic selfishness of the great nations, does not absolve the statesmen of the world from nature's obligation to form such a federal world government. Their refusal to obey this obvious law of human nature has ever had, and ever will entail, nature's sanction of the horrors of needless wars, of which all nations are guilty. "And the path of peace they have not known" (Rom. 3:17).

The first four of President Woodrow Wilson's "Fourteen Points" for international peace were ridiculed as naïve by Europeans, who soon wept tears of blood over their disregard.

---

12 *Phil.*, 2, 44.

Open covenants of peace openly arrived at.

Freedom of navigation outside territorial waters alike in peace and in war.

The removal, as far as possible, of economic barriers and the establishment of an equality of trade conditions among the nations.

Adequate guarantees given and taken that national armaments will be reduced to the lowest point consistent with domestic safety.

These are not merely points of treaty for administration of material affairs. They are the dictates of love among nations, and the only "paths of peace," which, according to Pius XI (*Quadragesimo Anno*),

have the principal foundation of stability in the mutual bond of minds and hearts, whereby the members are united with one another. If this bond is lacking, the best of regulations come to naught, as we have learned by too frequent experience. True cooperation will be possible for a single common good, only when the constituent parts of society feel themselves members of one great family and children of the same heavenly Father. . . .

True, our nature and our nature's God intend us to preserve our human rights; but they intend that only in emergency, when established authority cannot be appealed to, may one use violence in the preservation of his rights, and then only when the right preserved warrants the violence used. Love of humanity's social welfare requires that conflicts be submitted to courts, as the litigants are not fit judges in their own cause. One of the government's reasons for existence is to preserve the common good of society by judging and settling conflicts between individuals and groups over rights.

A peace is of a nature of a conquest;
For then both parties nobly are subdued
And neither party loser.[13]

This aim of the World Movement for World Federal Government was encouraged by Pope Pius XII (April 6, 1951):

Your movement dedicates itself to realizing an effective political organization of the world. Nothing is more in conformity with the

---

[13] 2 *Henry IV*, 4, 2, 89.

traditional doctrine of the Church, nor better adapted to her teaching concerning legitimate and illegitimate warfare, especially in the present circumstances. It is necessary to arrive at an organization of this kind, if for no other reason than to put a stop to the armaments race. You are in harmony with the principles of political and social life so firmly founded and sustained by the Church.

For the sake of precious liberty, government should allow and aid litigants to settle their conflict amicably between themselves; but if they cannot or will not, government's serious duty is to enforce a peaceful settlement by impartial arbitration, suppressing any use of violence by the parties at variance. Violence in a decision of rights is immoral because it is irrational. Force does not prove who is right; it proves only who is stronger. Right is not established by might — bodily, financial, political, or military. Unless violence to decide conflict is banned between groups within nations, we are certainly not going to have peace between nations. Charity must begin at home; only then will it go abroad. National governments must first effectually suppress all violence and forestall all domestic warfare of strikes, lockouts, feuds, lynching, ku kluxery, organized boycotts, and hindrance of the exercise of rights, such as that of voting. Only when we have established the peace of love in our own house, can we make peace with other houses. The difference between relatively small domestic wars within a nation and wars between nations is that the mobs in international wars are large, mobs being understood as groups that attain their ends by violence.

Given a government that is responsible, as it should be, all violent conflict between groups and nations is irrational and immoral. Would we judge as moral and according to the social nature of man that each family in a nation must defend its rights with machine guns? Such a situation between nations is not less immoral and contrary to the nature of man. It is not less vicious and abnormal for nations to settle their conflict by war than it is for one city to go to war with another.

It is to be expected that governments will wish to settle international difference by war when they allow industrial, racial, and religious war to be their national spirit. This malfeasance of government is the certain preparation for violent totalitarian rule.

Accustoming the people to attaining their aims by war is well styled by the Prussian General von Clausewitz (1780–1831) as "the act of violence to force our opponent to do our will"; with whom the British Lord Fisher agrees: "The essence of war is violence. Moderation in war is imbecility."

Cromwell was deluded when he told Parliament (September 4, 1654): "It is material interest that keeps peace." The adoration of the golden calf of commerce, set up as the idol of the nation, demands that love, good will, and justice repeatedly be sacrificed in its worship. For this reason, commerce has been the chief instigator of "war, the son of hell" (Shakespeare).

To seek peace means, according to Pope Benedict XV, "to strive in every way that the charity of Jesus Christ should rule supreme among men." "Pax Romana" is not Italian peace; it is the "Pax Christi," whose Vicar resides at Rome. The Church has the commission from Christ to bring peace: "When you come into a house, salute it. If then that house be worthy, your peace will come upon it" (Mt. 10:12).

The opposition of the devil to peace is expressed by Milton's demon declaring that he will infect mankind with his spirit of war:

Manslaughter shall be held the highest pitch
Of human glory.[14]

Christ began his redemption of the world at a time when it was at peace. He brought, as the heavenly heralds announced, "on earth peace among men of good will" (Lk. 2:14); and still, standing in the midst of them, He says: "Peace to you. It is I" (*ibid.* 24:36); "for he himself is our peace" (Eph. 2:14). Continued redemption by the Mystical Christ, the Church, requires peace between peoples and peace in each people.

May St. Augustine's experience of Christianity's increasing dominance of love in the world's history be ours.

It is love that is now renewing the nations. Overspreading the whole world, from the universal race of man it is making and gathering together a new people, the (Mystical) Body of the newly-married spouse of the Only-begotten Son of God. . . .[15]

14 *Paradise Lost,* 11, 691.
15 *In Joan.* tr. 15, 1.

II. LOVE THY GOD

I. HUMAN AND DIVINE LOVE OF GOD

1. *To Live Is to Love*

Every act of life is a desire, a wanting, an act of love. To act is to love; to live is to love. "Whoever lives true life will live true love" (E. Browning, *Aurora Leigh*). As electromagnetism is thought to be the one common power beneath all forms of material power, so love, whatever be its object, love for good or ill, is the one common fundamental motive power beneath all human motion of mind or body. "As the weights give movement to all the moving parts of a clock," says St. Francis de Sales, "so love gives to the soul all the movement it has."

"Love," says Shelley, "is the guide, the rule, the interpretation of Dante's mysticism. . . . At the consummation of his vision, the poet beholds, by penetrative intuition into the divine Light, how it is that love thus binds the universe into one, to make it resemble the Supreme Unity":

> . . . I saw combined,
> Bound by love within one volume,
> All the pages scattered through the world,
> Substance and accident and their conditions,
> So merged one into the other
> That what I saw in many words was but one light.[1]

Only love of the Infinite, such as Dante's, can unify in symphony the many discordant loves of man.

Love, in God, is the teeming fount from which all the rivulets of created loves take their rise. "The Creator of the universe," observes Origen, "when He formed you, deposited in your heart the seeds of

[1] *Paradiso,* canto 33, v. 85–105.

love."[2] God the Creator calls Himself the very substance Love. The image, then, of God in creatures must be love: love of God, love of self, love of others. "Love," as Bossuet aptly notes, "is the spirit of return to God."

Our hounding spirit courses through the forest of life panting after satisfaction of its love. The very being and nature of God demands that, for Him, to give being to creatures is to give them loves, inclinations, instincts, tendencies; for to be is to love. Enmeshed in one universal whole, these tendencies of creatures are the active expression of their unity, in the universal end which they achieve.

St. Augustine's far-reaching mind was captivated by the contemplation of the inciting tendencies, both human and nonhuman, as the unifying source of the universe's activities, which he called their loves:

> Fire tends on high. The stone tends downward. They are impelled by their gravities. They seek their proper places. . . . Things that are not well ordered are restless. Order them and they are at peace. . . .
> My gravitation is my love. By it I am carried wherever I am carried. We are fired by Thy Gift (the Holy Spirit); and we are carried on high. We are enkindled, and we rise.[3]

Man is a complex of loves, of seekings. Like the goddess of India with many arms, he reaches out for satisfaction of many and conflicting instincts, which are the prime movers of his activity. Since man, out of all things, has unnatural as well as natural loves — tendencies which further or hurt the general good of his nature and God's extrinsic glory in him — he has been necessarily equipped with free choice to determine intelligently which of his outreachings he will satisfy and to what extent, and which he will partially or wholly deny. "Man's life," says ancient Job, "is a warfare," a warfare of conflicting loves seeking satisfaction at the expense of frustration of other loves. The loves, or instincts, which one habitually satisfies and the loves which he habitually frustrates determine what his "character" is.

Nonhuman beings always tend to their real good without choice.

2 *Hom. in Cant.* 2, 9; *PG* 13, 55.
3 *Confessions*, 2, 9.

There is no mistaking evil for good in them. The resultant of forces in physics, the affinities in chemistry, and the biological tendencies in plants and animals determine their action inevitably, without fail and without choice. But for man, "there are no galley slaves in the royal vessel of divine love." So says St. Francis de Sales. "Every man works his oar voluntarily." "Where the Spirit of the Lord is there is freedom" (2 Cor. 3:17), freedom to choose the love of God.

Liberty of love is the goal of the *Exercises* of St. Ignatius, who entitles them: "Spiritual Exercises to regulate one's Life, without allowing oneself to be ruled by any disorderly tendency." Conversion to a fervent spiritual life is the attainment of liberty, love making us free. All liberty must be under law; and perfect liberty must be under the perfect law of love.

The *Exercises* seek to have us rise to the supremest possible love of God, that is, to the supremest possible liberty of the soul dominating its tendencies. We first consider the freeing of ourselves with the help of grace from mortal and venial sin; then, as far as possible, from the least imperfection in love arising from the thrall of ungenerous tendencies. "Indifference," so strongly inculcated by Loyola, is freedom of spirit from all that is not God's will. The state of a really free man is in his use of creatures *tantum quantum,* only inasmuch as they serve his love of Christ, so that they do not rule him.

Through the *Exercises* we are to "go in peace," freed from any undue attachment, as Zaccheus, after his association with Christ, was freed from his slavery to money. The "election" of a program for our future life is the election of total freedom in total love of Christ, a freedom antipodal to the freedom of the brutal Nietzsche, or of the greedy hedonist, or of the "anguished" existentialist, all of which yearned-for freedoms are complete slavery to personal passions. Love is the liberty needed to say in the "Suscipe" of the *Exercises:* "Take, O Lord, and receive my liberty."

Love must be free; for only free actions are strictly human actions, the realization of our full selves. In delivering our free actions to God by accommodating them to His will, we deliver to Him our whole selves in the fullest of giving. So powerful is love in the will to do God's will that an act, which is otherwise not God's will, becomes His will through the love of God in the one who freely

chooses it as His will. Such is the case of the soldier who mistakenly
believes it noble and God's will to commit suicide rather than be
taken prisoner. His suicide, a crime in itself, becomes a consummate
act of love of God because it is freely chosen as such.

2. *Love Is the Homing Instinct*

Developing Augustine's view of love as the quest of all creatures for
their end or good, Aquinas teaches: "In each of these tendencies
love is said to be that which is the cause of their movement toward
their loved end."[4] In truth, observes Cardinal Mercier:

> that which is deepest in the nature of every creature is precisely
> its inclination toward the absolute Good. The law which governs
> its action, whether it be carried out unconsciously or obeyed in
> full knowledge, is the impression on the creature of the one
> Primary Love.[5]

All finite reality has a homing instinct. The material creature is
no sooner real than it yields to its gravitation toward God, through
its finite reflection of Him in its total being, in its total activity, in
its totally fulfilled purpose which is in the mind of its Creator.
Man, in his material element, also orients himself immediately,
entirely, constantly, to God in the same way. In his spiritual nature,
man must also return, but freely, to his Maker by fulfillment of
God's purpose for him and by his consequent supernatural possession of God. Creatures are the echo of the Creative Voice. The echo,
man, is to answer its Word freely, in love of its source.

A baby yearns for air to breathe, although it does not know what
air is. Man's being hungers no less for God, even when he does not
know God. Our fundamental necessity is God, although it must be
realized in our freely chosen love of Him. What, then, is the first
word in Christianity? "Thou shalt love!" What is the first word in
social relations, familial, national, and international? "Thou shalt
love!" Man was made for nothing else than love, however you look

[4] *Summa* 1-2, 21, 1, c, *et passim.*
[5] *Conferences,* Transl. O'Kavanagh, Westminster, Md., 1943, p. 108.

upon him. He does nothing but love. He is what his love is: noble or ignoble. The investment of one's heart is the most important business of man, far more precarious than the investment of one's fortune.

As sugar is sweet in itself and sweetens all other foods, so love of God is holy in itself and makes all other actions holy. If I have a great love of God, I am great. If I have small love of Him, I am small. If I have no love of God, I am, as St. Paul says, nothing. Love of God is in a way like artistic talent. Not the hours of work, nor the size or number of one's paintings determines their merit, praise, or return in money. Not the length of life nor the notability or multitude of actions performed, but the intensity of the love of God in performing them, whatever they may be, determines their glory to God and their merit.

All evil is perverted love. Perhaps this was what Beaudelaire sensed when he saw divine love under the masquerade of perverted loves: "I have treasured the form and essence divine of my decomposed loves." Juliana of Norwich in her *Revelations of Divine Love* receives "in ghostly understanding" the significance and purpose of human and supernatural life:

> What? Wouldst thou wit thy Lord's meaning in this thing? Wit it well. Love was his meaning. Who sheweth it to thee? Love. Wherefore sheweth He it thee? For love. Hold thee therein, thou shalt wit more in the same. But thou shalt never wit more other without end.

> "Love, therefore! Fill the fugitive hour with love!"
>
> (Lamartine, *Le Lac.*)

Love of God is the center in which all the radii of the circle of life converge. So the human God taught us (Mt. 22:36–38). As the soul, with its mind, will, and emotions, gives the sacred worth to the lowly clay that is man, as the thought contained is the meaning and worth of the pregnant word, so the meaning and depth of the love of God is the meaning and depth of every life. All lives are purses of various textures, but all made to contain the same sole wealth, love of God.

Creature love has, as its parents, riches and poverty. Love is a king and a beggar. The tendency to love is born of riches; the tendency to be loved is born of poverty. One is active, one is passive, as the creature's nature is both active, giving good, and passive, receiving good. God's creative love of His creatures and His desire to be loved by man are identical. Both are filled by His giving good to His creatures, not by receiving good from them, somewhat as air tends to be sought by a vacuum and to fill a vacuum itself. If it is true that one loves another for that which is lacking in oneself, then no love has the stimulus of the love of infinite Good.

Love is a unitive power. It is the active-passive nature of human love that both produces and receives union with another active-passive human love. Our love of God and union with Him is wholly passive, in the sense that we receive union with Him but do not produce it. His love of us is totally active in giving to His creatures. Full love in itself has all goods and not only wishes but also gives all goods to the beloved. God's love alone not only wishes all goods fit for our nature but also has and gives them, inasmuch as the receptivity of our love meets them. All human love, therefore, tends, usually implicitly, to love that infinite Good wherein it attains all that it is possible for it to love. Water is sweeter the farther it flows. The water of which Christ speaks, which alone can slake our thirst to love and be loved, flows an infinite distance, coming to us from God.

3. The Bond of Perfection

Love of God is so obviously and fundamentally the law of human nature that we find it commanded long before the era of the supernatural religion of Christ.

> The Lord thy God will circumcise thy heart, and the heart of thy seed: that thou mayest love the Lord thy God with all thy heart and with all thy soul, that thou mayest live. . . . This commandment, that I command thee this day is not above thee, nor far off from thee. . . . But the word is very nigh unto thee, in thy mouth and in thy heart, that thou mayest do it (Deut. 30:6, 11, 14).

Because of their very human nature, then, adults have a grave obligation to make an act of love of God for what He is, probably at least once a year,[6] certainly oftener than once in five years. Both naturally and supernaturally, "Charity rightly disposes man with regard to his ultimate end."[7] St. Thomas holds that, when the budding mind first recognizes God as its purpose of existence, it is gravely obliged to acknowledge Him as such and to make an act of love of God.[8]

"One must get rid of the false notion," admonishes Cardinal Billot,[9] "which is a residue of Jansenism, that it is very difficult to make an act of perfect love. How utterly false this is, is clear from the fact that this act is contained within the scope of ordinary grace, since it is imposed by a commandment binding on all."

Of all the early teachers of the Church, St. Augustine is most emphatic as to the need of this supernatural love in human life:

> The love of God, by which one attains to God, cannot come except from God the Father, by Jesus Christ with the Holy Spirit. Through this love of the Creator, one uses creatures well; without this love of the Creator, one abuses every creature.[10]

Augustine does not mean that we must make an explicit act of love in each action, in order that it be supernaturally good. As long as an action is done under an habitual attitude, or "virtual intention," as a consequence of a former act of love of God, it is supernaturally good and meritorious. In this way, a bookkeeper at work virtually performs an act of love of his dear family in every computation that he makes, although he does not explicitly think of them in doing each act. This "virtual" direction of our actions into the love of God fulfills Augustine's instruction:

> The rule of love is that you direct to God all your thoughts, all your life, all your intelligence, to the God from whom you hold that which you direct to Him.[11]

St. Paul (1 Cor. 12) enumerates the marvelous charismata or miraculous gifts of the early Christians, and then declares that he proposes a much more valuable and higher attainment: love of God,

---

[6] Denz. 1156, 1157, 1289.
[7] Aquinas, *De carit.*, 5, c.
[8] *Summa*, 1-2, 89, 6, c.

[9] *De virt. infus, ed.* 3, 435.
[10] *Contra Jul.* 4, 3, 33; *PL* 44, 756.
[11] *Christian Doctrine* 1, 2, 21; *PL* 34, 27.

which includes and animates love of the neighbor — love, which is
grace's so fundamental virtue that some theologians have less exactly
considered grace and love of God identical — love which St. Paul calls
"the bond of perfection" (Col. 3:14), or better translated according
to commentators (cf. Knabenbauer), "the perfect bond" of union of
the soul with God and with the neighbor in the Mystical Body. On
this love, St. Paul (1 Cor. 13) gives us his classic lyric:

> If I should speak with the tongues of men and of angels, but do not
> have charity, I am become as sounding brass or a tinkling cymbal.
> And if I have prophecy and know all mysteries and all knowledge,
> and if I have all faith so as to remove mountains, yet do not have
> charity, I am nothing. And if I distribute all my goods to feed
> the poor, and if I deliver my body to be burned, yet do not have
> charity, it profits me nothing (1–3).

This last sentence makes it clear that Paul is speaking of love of
God, saying that, unless love of our neighbor as "social service" is
love of God, it is worthless. Then the Apostle outlines the moral
beauties with which love is adorned and the moral deformities
which are absent from love:

> Charity is patient, is kind; charity does not envy, is not pre-
> tentious, is not puffed up, is not ambitious, is not self-seeking, is
> not provoked; thinks no evil, does not rejoice over wickedness, but
> rejoices with the truth; bears with all things, believes all things,
> endures all things (4–7).

Love, he says, is immortal; and all charismata will cease and give
place to love in heaven, which is their very purpose:

> Charity never fails, whereas prophecies will disappear, and tongues
> will cease, and knowledge will be destroyed. . . . So, there abide
> faith, hope and charity, these three; but the greatest of these is
> charity (8, 13).

Paul's direction of the Corinthian Christians: "Aim after charity"
(1 Cor. 14:1) means that we must drive after love of God as a businessman drives after money, or as an ambitious man pursues fame. The
Apostle totalizes (ibid. 16:4) all good actions urged on the Corinthians
in his exhortation that all their actions be done in supernatural love
of God, that is, through grace. Carry out all your activities in love,
he tells the Ephesians, so that your persons and lives are "rooted

and grounded in love" (3:17). His prayer for the Philippians is
"that your charity may more and more abound in knowledge and
all discernment" (1:9).

Love of God is a good beyond all price; and all other goods are
reduced to it, so the Apostle assures us: "For those who love God
all things work together unto good" (Rom. 8:28). Literally true of
the love of God is the hyperbole: "For him that has love and no
more, there is nothing more to have."

Perfection is any action done in full love. Love wholly, and you
win in a moment what hardly is won in a life. Hence Augustine's
well-known axiom: "Love and do what you will"; for whatever you
do will be perfect. "Let there be interiorly the root of love," he
says, "and from that root can come only good."[12] Love simply is
perfection.

A man is better as his love is greater. If one asks if a man is
good, he does not ask what he believes or what he hopes for, but
what he loves. He who loves as he ought to love believes undoubtedly and hopes as he ought to.[13]

"Holiness," he says "will be complete when love is complete";[14]
and again: "Where there is love, what can be wanting? Where love
is missing, what can be of any use?"[15] He explains that it is love
which is the physical impossibility of sinning in heaven, as it is our
moral impossibility of sinning on earth.[16] To sin we must cease to love.

Rivaling St. Augustine in extolling love of God, St. John Climacus,
the most popular of eastern ascetics, followed the many ecclesiastical
teachers before him in making love the likening of man to God, in
which consists holiness and the glory of God. Evagrius of Pontus, an
early eastern ascetic of the fourth century, teaches: "The role of love
is to establish in us the likeness of God."[17] Truly, since we become
in a way that which we love, St. Gregory teaches that "through love
we become in a certain sense that which God is";[18] we become
divinized. So also St. Maximus of the seventh century, eminent

12 *1 Jn.* 7, 8; *PG* 35, 2033.
13 *Enchiridion* 117; *PL* 40, 286.
14 *De perfect. just.* 3, 8; *PL* 44, 2033.
15 *In Joan* 83, 3; *PL* 35, 1846.
16 *De civitat. Dei* 23, 30, 3; *PL* 41, 802.
17 *Practica*, 1, 61; *PG* 40, 1236.
18 *In Eccles.* hom. 8; *PG* 44, 737.

eastern mystical writer: "Love makes men gods."[19] "God justifies the
wicked," St. Augustine says, "not only by forgiving his sin but by
giving him love."[20]

4. Love of God Above All Else

The full course of any true human love runs thus: We love our
neighbor by willing a good for him, such as education, because it
is his well-being. We will the well-being of our neighbor, because
such willing is the perfecting of our own social nature. We will this
perfecting of our nature, because thereby we perfect our reflection
of God in our nature and action. We will this perfecting of God's
reflection in our nature, because we are thus the glory of God, which
He intends in us and which brings us eternal beatitude. Beatitude is
a further reflection of God and His further glory in us. We will
His glory in us, because we love, with a love of complacence and
friendship, the infinite nature and will which are thus glorified.
Thus, this reason, the "formal" motive, the unitary ground, leads us
up on a logical stairway, through all loves to the complacent love of
God. "God is not truly God," says the ardent St. Basil, "for those
who do not love Him."

It is hard to know or to express absolutely the degree of our love
of God; but we can know it to be supreme when we express it
relatively: "more than all else." The degree of our love for Him is
made plain by the greatness of other goods, which, with His grace,
we are ready to deny ourselves, in a choice between Him and them.
This was the devil's test of Job's love of God, to whom he cynically
remarks: "Stretch forth thy hand a little, and touch [ruin] all that
he hath, and see if he blesseth thee not to thy face" (1:11; cf.
Hummelauer's commentary). The difficulty of an action done for
the beloved expresses the degree of sacrifice which we are ready to
make for the beloved. This is signified in the mandate to love God
"with all thy strength."

We are commanded by the Creator in the Natural Law, by

---

[19] *Epist.* 2 ad Joan. cub.; *PG* 91, 393; *De carit.* 4, 20.
[20] *Op. impref. contra Jud.* 2; *PL* 45, 1212.

Yahweh in the Old Law, and by Christ in the New Law to love Him with our whole heart and with all our forces. This means that there is to be no other love of our heart which is not also love of God, no other action of our human powers that is not also an act of love of God. Platonic astronomy held that the highest heaven made all the lower heavens and earth follow its motion. Love of God is the highest love above human loves, and it should govern the motion of all of them.

Hence mystics call full love of God a "marriage" of the soul with God, in which no other good is loved unless in it the soul finds expression of its love of God, just as the loving wife sacrifices all loves of other men which are not in accord with love of her husband. The Absolute Good must be absolute Master of the soul with which it is married. St. Bonaventure teaches that the more independent loves we have, the more complex we are. The fewer the objects that divide our love, the simpler and stronger is our life. But we may have the unity and strength of one love manifested in the loves of many objects. Such is God's one simple love for Himself which is manifested in His love for His myriad creatures.

The Beloved Disciple teaches (1 Jn. 4:10) that we love God because God loves us first. The fountain of all love is God, who from the source of His love for Himself derives the stream of His love for us, which in turn gives us our love for God and all our real love for creatures. Like Him, we love Him and ourselves in our love of others. Thus all real loves are from the same creation of His love, duly turning back to their Creator.

The beginning of all things must be their end. Love, "reacheth therefore from end to end mightily, and ordereth all things sweetly" (Wisd. 8:1). Love's "going out is from the end of heaven, and his circuit even to the end thereof: and there is no one that can hide himself from his heat" (Ps. 18:7).

Love of God does not close itself up in isolation; it brings into its house the real loves of all persons and things. Luis de Leon tells a story of a certain fruit tree in Persia that has delicious and health-giving fruit; but when it is planted outside of its native region, its fruit is poisonous.[21] Love of creatures, which grows in Christ, is

---

[21] *Nombres de Cristo,* 1, 2.

wholesome food for our souls; planted outside of Him, its proper habitat, it turns to poison.

Supernatural love of God, love of God above all else, is graciously friendly toward all human loves that deserve the name. Our inevitable love of self and of others is not necessarily a rival to supernatural love of God, which assumes and suffuses right human love, as light assumes and suffuses the morning air.

When spiritual writers say that love of God does not permit other loves of the soul, they speak of loves opposed, either wholly or partly, to the love of God. Other loves, which are phases of the love of God or compatible with it, are aids to loving God. They must, however, be watched and guided so that they do not develop in themselves any opposition to or disregard of God. All loves, which are not love of God are, with apologies to Shakespeare, "the fool of time." Love of God must always have the last word.

Love of God "above all else" sounds and is magnificent precisely because it is so rational, so fact-facing. It is difficult to be a wholly rational being; in fact, it is impossible for a notable time without the supernatural aid of grace; and in love of God above all else, rationality attains its apex of perfection. Since we are absolutely sure, by faith and reason, that God is infinitely all the good that we can love outside of Him, it is basic common sense to love Him above all other good.

We are to love the beauty and wealth of the creature because it is the mere image of the wealth and beauty of God; and we must love the image always because of that which it images. He who loves God above all else will not be enslaved by his love of creatures; he will be able to walk through the fire of total love, not only without a sense of loss, but with a sense of sovereign enrichment.

St. Augustine asks: "What do I love when I love Thee, my God?" and he answers:

> I love, in a way, light, sound, fragrance, food, an embrace, when I love my God, who is light, sound, fragrance, food and embrace for my interior man — when he shines forth to my soul who is not confined by place, when He sounds who is not stilled by time, when He is fragrance who is not dispersed by the wind, when He is savor who is not lessened by greediness, when He remains who

becomes not tiresome by ennui. This is what I love when I love my God.[22]

As long as one has understanding of the good that God is, and as long as he has free choice, he can readily, with ever available grace, love God more than himself and more than all other goods that can give him satisfaction. He *is* our real good, infinitely and solely. Dryden entitled a play: "All for Love, or The World Well Lost." The play in which we are cast has been entitled by God: "All for the Love of God, or The World Well Gained"; for in love of God, we have also all the values of the world.

5. *Love of God As Our Ultimate End*

This expression means, first, that the *object* of our love, God glorified and possessed by us, is the ultimate purpose of our existence. He is the one supreme purpose of all our minor purposes. It means, second, that our *action* of loving God is the supreme end and value of all other actions of our existence. No creature is the ultimate object of our love, even spouse, children, or friends, and much less, wealth, honor, or pleasure. All of them have their significance and worth, all of them should be loved, but only as means of glorifying, loving, and possessing God. To love God as our ultimate end is the same as to love Him "for His own sake."

This was expressed by God when He commanded: "Thou shalt love the Lord, thy God, with thy whole heart" and when He asserted, as He did a decade of times through the inspired writers, "I am a jealous God" — that is, I must be your principal love in all your loves of creatures. From the fact that by His very nature He must be the only God, He logically demands that we love Him with our whole heart:

Hear, O Israel, the Lord our God is one Lord. Thou shalt love the Lord thy God with thy whole heart (Deut. 6:4–5).

***

[22] *Confessions,* 10, 6, 8.

Christ assumed this teaching of the Old Testament and reinforced it, making it "the first commandment of all." His interlocutor Scribe understood Him and replied:

> Well answered, Master, thou hast said truly that he is one and that there is no other besides him; and that he should be loved with the whole heart, and with the whole understanding, and with the whole soul, and with one's whole strength. . . . Jesus, seeing that he had answered wisely, said to him: "Thou art not far from the kingdom of God" (Mk. 12:32–34).

God's quest of man's undivided love, which loves nothing in which he does not love God, is the epitome of the Old Testament with its insistence that there is only one God and that there is no other God who could divide our love: "The Lord he is God, and there is no other besides him" (Deut. 4:35; cf. also 4:39; 6:14; Isa. 44:6).

God cannot go against the truth of the uniqueness that He is and against the truth of the total love due to Him because of His uniqueness. Hence, He must of necessity be "a jealous God," admitting no rival God who deserves to divide love for Him:

> Thou shalt not have strange gods before me. . . . I am the Lord, thy God, mighty, jealous (Exod. 20:5).
> Adore not any strange god. The Lord his name is Jealous, he is a jealous God (*ibid.* 34:14).
> The Lord thy God is a consuming fire, a jealous God (Deut. 4:24; cf. 6:15).

There can be no conflict between the good that is God and our real good. St. Teresa of Avila and some others, in the intensity of their love of God, made an impossible supposition when they declared that they were ready to go to hell for love of God. The very reason and "formal object" of our love of God is His infinite Goodness or worth, both to us and in Himself, says St. Thomas: "Charity attends to the motive of loving, the divine Goodness."[23] God made, and must make, our nature to imitate His divine nature, in its fundamental natural tendency to possess the Good that He is. To make the supposition of forfeiting that Good freely, out of love of that Good, is as impossible as to be ready to hate God out of love of God.

---

[23] *Summa,* 2–2, 23, 5.

"Perfection in love of God," says St. Augustine, "approaches the intensity of total disregard of self."[24] And according to St. Gregory, with many other early Christian writers, "we progress in the love of God when we completely go out of ourselves."[25] They must be understood as speaking of self inasmuch as it is contrary to love of God. Psychologically it is impossible to discard love of self; for in all loving, since we are thereby fulfilling a tendency, we must love ourselves. Love of ourselves is proposed by our Lord as our norm for love of our neighbor: "Thou shalt love thy neighbor as thyself." Irregular love of self, which spiritual guides condemn, is really hatred of oneself. So St. Augustine made his frequently noted assertion to God: "He loves Thee not who loves something with Thee, which he does not love because of Thee."[26]

"The world, the flesh, and the devil" can be simply reduced to our own immoral tendencies to them. To love God above all else is in effect to love God above any satisfaction of these immoral tendencies. When spiritual writers advise that we should not love ourselves if we would love God, they mean simply that we must not love our satisfaction more than we love God, which is to harm ourselves since God is the satisfaction for which we are made. In other words, we must not prefer our will to His will which is all-beneficent and our sole welfare. Again, when they write that we must not seek our own glory but the glory of God, they would have us seek our real glory which is God's glory.

We are like a son running his father's business. He does not work for himself, for all profit goes to his father. But he is heir to the business; and all that he does for his father's interests is for his own interest. He is not justified in managing the business exclusively for his own present profit, disregarding his father's profit, in which alone he can find his own profit. On this love of God "with thy whole heart" Augustine writes:

> See if God wishes to allow in you that you love even yourself. . . .
> What remains of thy heart with which to love thyself? What part
> of thy soul? "With the whole," He says. He demands the whole
> of thee who made thee. . . .

---

[24] *Serm.* 143, 3, *et al.*
[25] *Moralia* 22, 20, 46.
[26] *Confessions,* 10, 290.

For if God is the supreme good of man, which you cannot deny, it follows plainly that to seek the Supreme Good is to live well. . . . In this way love is preserved unspoiled and integral, which is temperance; that love is not broken by difficulties, which is fortitude; that love serves no one else but God, which is justice; and that love is vigilant in deciding matters, which is prudence. This love is man's one perfection, by which alone he begs that he may enjoy the sincerity of truth.[27]

Good persons not infrequently fail in love of God with their whole heart by loving those whom God, indeed, wills them to love, but whom they love more or otherwise than God wills, as St. Francis de Sales deprecates:

The love of our parents, friends, benefactors, is good in itself when it is in accord with God's will; yet we can love them excessively. Like our occupations, be they never so spiritual, so our exercises of devotion may be loved inordinately, as when we prefer them before obedience, or before a more general good, or when we love them as though they were the purpose of our existence, while they are only means and furtherances to our ultimate intention, which is divine love.[28]

6. "I Am He Whom Thou Seekest"

In loving any finite good we love a being more that has more of that good. Our tendency then is implicitly to God, who is all that is good without limit and without defect. Philosophically we call this love of the All-Good "the love of being," that is, love of all that is within the compass of the word *being*. Elizabeth Browning uses this idea to express her full love in *How do I love Thee?*

>   I love thee to the depth and breadth and height
>   My soul can reach, when feeling out of sight
>   For the ends of being and ideal grace.

Since, by nature, I must love the good that I am, I must naturally, with far greater necessity and reasonableness, implicitly love God

[27] *De mor. eccl.* 1, 25; *PL* 32, 1330.
[28] *The Love of God*, 10, 4.

who is infinitely all that I am; and I must strive to make this love more and more explicit.

Sauer, the German ornithologist,[29] has demonstrated how birds, such as the warblers of Scandinavia, at a definite, exact time, have an impelling instinct to migrate, and that they have a built-in compass which they must follow. The stars are their guide while they do their weeks of flying, usually at night, after which they arrive at a definite spot in southern Africa, every year. These ¾ ounce warblers fly alone and unerringly the first time, even when they have been hatched and raised, up to the time of migration, indoors and out of sight of the sky. Birds thus migrate from northern Canada to the dot of land in the mid-Pacific that is Hawaii.

We are, as it were, migrating birds, with a built-in urge to fly during a number of years to the definite infinite Good. But we freely follow, as we can freely disregard, our compass of instinctive love of God, which is guided by heaven. We must strive to render this unconscious, instinctive tendency to the unexperienced infinite Good as conscious and as expressly chosen as it can be. All persons love God above any other thing, and above all things all together, but only radically, objectively, and unconsciously. If they had the vision and direct knowledge of what God is, they would, indeed, unavoidably love Him above all else, perfectly, subjectively, and explicitly. Hence, St. Augustine addresses God, "God, whom everything loves that can love, whether aware or unaware of it."[30]

The one searching for a hidden treasure chest implicitly loves much more a larger treasure chest, if he only knew about it. In our love of any good, real or only apparent, we implicitly love God much more, who is infinitely that good. It is this inevitable love of God which we have consciously in heaven and which we are to approach on earth voluntarily and with effort, through reason and faith. If we love the copper coin that the creature is, all the more should we love the golden coin that the Creator is.

St. Gregory the Great tells us that our love of God must be totalitarian, because even all that love is too little, and any love less than that is totally incongruous: "No measure to our love of

---

[29] *Scientific American*, 199, 2, pp. 42–47.
[30] *Soliloq.* 1, 2; *PL* 32, 869.

God is indicated by Christ, because true measure for the love of God is to love Him without measure."[31] "One does not fittingly enclose God within a barrier" by measured love of Him, advises Pope St. Leo,[32] like St. John Damascene, for whom love of God is "a continual driving of the soul beyond its powers." There is no temperance or moderation to be exercised in love of God. In love of God it is not true that "happiness is found in moderation." Happiness is in the love of God, and without limit; the more that love is, the more is our happiness. Here there is no "happy median."

"I know, my soul, that love is thy life," muses Hugo of St. Victor in *The Earnest of the Soul.* Infinitely good and wise Creator, God has necessarily made possible for man that which will satisfy his many loves and fulfill the endless ever increasing yearning and seeking of his activity. Unless creature loves are also love of God carrying out His will in them, it is only too true, as pessimists say, that human loves are children of illusion and parents of disillusion. But it is unthinkable that God could have created man, the greatest of His visible creatures, to be the greatest of frustrations by giving him insatiable desires only to mock him. Thirst without water, sight without light, mind without truth were not a tithe of the frustration of human love without the infinite Good to satisfy it.

All love, except the love of God, is unsatisfied, a drinking of sea water to allay burning thirst. All loves are to tell us of love of the divine of which they are shadows. "In every good desired we desire the Supreme Good," says St. Augustine. In all loves the invisible "tremendous Lover" speaks:

> Ah, blindest, fondest, weakest,
> I am He whom thou seekest.
> (Thompson, *The Hound of Heaven*)

Once we totally long for the Beloved, we are united with Him; once we realize that we are hastening on a journey to Him, we have arrived; once we are aware that our existence is only the seeking of Him, we have found Him. When we acknowledge our leprosy, we are whole; when we cry out that we are blind, we begin

---

[31] *Moralia* 10, 6, 8.
[32] *Serm.* 48, 3.

to see. "In that thou hast sought Me, thou hast found Me," is the assurance of Absolute Reality.

7. It Is No Longer I That Love

Christ is the only lover who actually dwells in the heart of the beloved. Human love, human appetite for satisfaction, has been, not merely increased, but transformed to supernatural powers of loving, by its assumption through grace into participation in God's own love. So Gardeil explains:

> The Holy Spirit does not cause in us the love of God, as an exterior agent which becomes foreign as soon as it has finished operating. He produces this love as an interior cause indwelling in it; for the Apostle says that "He has been given to us." His activity is like that of a soul, ever present in that which it does, whose operation never ceases. So long as the just soul loves God, it does not act alone. It has deep in its heart the Spirit of God; and it is this Spirit that causes the soul to utter, with all truth and efficacy the name of filial love: "My Father."[33]

As light suffuses the dark diamond, giving its fulfillment of incandescent splendor, which it could never have of itself, so grace suffuses man's natural capacity to love and elevates it to a participated divine capacity for satisfaction in the infinite Good. Grace is the supernatural quality of the soul and supernatural love is its basic activity.

Charity, in grace, loves God divinely; hence, it is not perfected by an increase of merely human love of God, somewhat as no increase of training can make an animal intellectual. The enhancing of supernatural love, or charity, is, and must be, increase of participation in God as divine love, the Holy Spirit. However, this supernatural love must be also a human love, as well as divine; for the more we are divine beings of grace, necessarily the more we are powerfully and exquisitely human beings.

---

[33] *Gifts of the Holy Ghost in the Dominican Saints,* p. 6.

There is more than man's loving in Christian love. In the same sense in which St. Paul declares (Gal. 2:20): "It is no longer I that live, but Christ lives in me," each of us may say, through grace, it is no longer I that love, but Christ loves in me. St. Augustine meditates on this transfusion of Christ's love into our own:

> By loving, man becomes a member (of Christ); and by love he fits into the structure of Christ's Body; and so, there will be one Christ loving Himself.[34]

For William of St. Thierry the love through which we love God is the Holy Spirit received in grace:

> Thou lovest Thyself in us; and Thou lovest us in Thee, since we love Thee through Thyself; and we are united with Thee, insofar as we merit to love Thee.[35]

Love in grace is the draught of divine life, divine power to love, divine Good to be loved, with which Christ intends to sate our thirsting souls: "If anyone thirst, let him come to me and drink" (Jn. 7:37). "He who drinks of the water that I will give him shall never thirst again" (Jn. 4:13; 6:35); "Drink, and be inebriated my dearly beloved" (Cant. 5:1). Come, drink of My heart's life and of its love in the sacraments, those veins of grace in the rock of sacramental signs, through which My life and love flow into your being, until such time as sacramental carriers shall be needed no more. Then I shall inebriate you directly in beatific experience of the flood of My life, love, and happiness, when you shall "drink of the torrent" of My pleasures (Ps. 35:9). In preparation for that time, according to St. Prosper: "That which we should love above all as our real selves, are the gifts of grace received from God, that is, supernatural love for God in us."[36]

---

[34] *In Epist. ad Parthos,* 10; *PL* 35, 2055.
[35] *On Contemplating God,* 7, 15; *PL* 84, 375.
[36] *The Vocation of All Peoples,* 1, 5, 6; *PL* 51, 651.

8. *"Open Thy Mouth Wide, and I Will Fill It"*
(Ps. 80:11)

God tells us through His psalmist that His love for us will be as great as we allow. The wider we open our heart, the more He will fill it with His love and grace. We should emulate the birdlings which open their mouth so wide to the mother feeding them that they seem to be only a mouth. God will match His divine generosity with our human generosity.

It is said that when St. Francis Xavier, as a professor of the Sorbonne in Paris, made the Spiritual Exercises for the first time, under St. Ignatius, he tied his hands and feet together. This was his symbol of complete surrender to God's will and pleasure which he so generously realized afterward. "Here I am," said those bonds. "Command me, O Lord, as You will; dispose of me as You will." He who has possession of our whole will has possession of our whole love, of our whole life, and of our whole person.

Magnificent generosity in love of God is not reserved only to the highly intellectual, or only to the mystical person. It is quite simple while wonderfully profound. That is why it is found in quite simple persons. It alone is achievement in any life. Positively, it is simply to do God's will as we know it and to accept God's arrangement of our circumstances and His effects on us through the world about us. That is all. But it encompasses all possible perfection and sanctity of living. Negatively, generosity is denial of our own will when it is not in accord with God's will. Both positively and negatively, generosity in love of God is love of Him above all else.

Human love of espousal insists that it be the only one really loving the beloved and the only one really loved by the beloved. It is fiercely exclusive love. But the more the soul espoused to God is loved by Him and loves Him, the more eager it is that others love Him and be loved by Him.

We must realize that all the blessed of heaven, whose whole life and sole life is love, look upon us with that intense concern which

arises from their total love of God's glory and from their individual
love of us, while from their midst the Sacred Heart of God speaks
to each of us personally: "My son, give me thy heart" (Prov. 23:26)
— the same Sacred Heart that on earth taught us: "Thou shalt love
the Lord thy God with thy *whole* heart."

To the one who loves God at all, this challenge to generosity is a
recurring storm; for those who make a yearly retreat it is a seasonal
storm, blowing in upon our spirit, the Pentecostal "violent wind
filling the whole house" of our lives, the wind (of the Spirit, Love)
blowing where it will (cf. Jn. 3:8). Do I bend before it like the
reed hugging the earth, until the demand for generosity is past, and
then rise again, my same self, swayed by every breeze? Or am I a tree
presenting full breast to love's salutary violence? It will not destroy
my happiness, as do many violent loves of time. It will shake my
character to its very roots; and thereby I shall grow deeper and
higher in my love of God and of my neighbor, although the storm
may blow away some of my weaker twigs and foliage.

The magnificent lover, St. Augustine, tells us his experience of
great love of God:

> God wants you rather than any gift from you. . . . You ask what
> you should offer to God: offer yourself. What does God seek from
> you except you? Among all earthly things He created nothing
> better than you. He seeks you from you because you had lost
> you. . . .
> If you do not give yourself, you lose yourself. . . . If you wish
> an estate, the seller says: Give me your gold. . . . Listen to what
> love says by the mouth of Wisdom: "Son, give Me thy heart." . . .
> It went ill with you when your heart was yours. . . . Make it Mine.
> You do not lose it. . . .[37]

God set total love as the goal of man. Nothing is too high for man
to aspire to; for there cannot be anything higher than total love of
God; and there will always be greater aspiration possible to love
with the aid of grace. Total love of God is, in a way, different for
each person; for each person has a different soul, mind, and heart,
while co-operating grace is always present to all for the accepting.
Augustine's love is with the whole of Augustine's mind, soul, and

---

[37] *Serm.* 82; 3; *PL* 38, 508; 48, 2; 4; *PL* 38, 212.

heart. A coolie's love of God is with the whole soul, mind, and heart
of a coolie. By grace, totality of love of God, befitting each one's
soul, mind, and heart, is possible to everyone.

No one, except the Blessed Virgin, ever reached his intended totality
of personal love of God; for we are by birth children of original sin,
although by grace of divine adoption we are the children of God.
We fail the imperious total demand of love, more or less. Love of
God is like human love: always uneasy. Love is joyful in what it is
and sad in what it is not. We find the saints in ecstasy of happiness
in their love of God and in ecstasy of suffering in the inadequacy of
their love. Out of the suffering love of Loyola came the motto for
his Society of Jesus: *"Ad majorem Dei gloriam!"* that is, "Seek the
greater glory of God."

The divine discontent of love seeks insatiably fuller and higher
expression. Love is not a temperate word. Since the degree of any and
of all virtue is the degree of love in it, there can never be excess in
love of God. In love, personal commitment is unconditioned, absolute,
and unlimited. As in electricity, the positive current of God's love
for us will always match the negative current of our love for Him.
If we are not totally in love with Him, we cannot have the totality
of participation in the Holy Spirit of Love intended for us. If we
are totally self-loving, we debar totally His munificent love for us;
we are left only with our poor selves; we deprive ourselves of the
reciprocity which all love seeks and which, in God alone, is infallibly
attained; we are incapable of that likeness to God which love
operates, and we remain only like our wretched selves; we remain
totally alone, who were intended by our nature and by Christianity
for the intimate communion of love of God. Without love of God,
we are crushed by the "anguish" of total aloneness which existential-
ists despairingly hold as the fundamental base of life.

Father J. N. Grou, S.J., proposed as our aim of life a love of God
which is "without admixture [of opposing loves], without division and
without reservation":

In French, as in Latin, there is no word to express more strongly
than *devouément* (dedication) the idea of close attachment, absolute determination of mind and heart to submit to all the wishes of
another, to anticipate what he wants, to make his interests one's

own, to give up all for him. . . . It adds thereto a consecration, in virtue of which the consecrated one is no longer his own, has no rights over himself and belongs wholly to the Supreme Being, to Whom he has devoted himself by the holiest and most irrevocable act of religion.[38]

High perfection, indeed, but it is only the rational exigency of the fact of what God is and of the fact of what we are. Grou avoids the unreal love of God which does not look for reward of happiness in heaven, a pitfall into which some previous French spiritual writers of note had stumbled:

> Like David, the soul serves God because of the reward; but the reward is only a secondary motive, while love is the first motive and most important. . . . One does not and cannot shut out self-interest . . . he establishes as his aim the glory that will be God's in the accomplishment of the divine will.[39]

In the mind of some Catholics, as in the mind of genuine Lutherans, the problem of life is simply: "Am I saved?" but the spirit of full Catholicism is not merely satisfaction in the hope of salvation; it includes dissatisfaction with oneself, the sense of a greater possible, but as yet unattained, love of God. "The love of Christ urges us"; we "feel the goad of love" impelling us the more as we advance in the love of God. Human law, when filled, is done with. The Catholic law of love is never entirely filled. We can fill a vessel perfectly, but we can never fill our life perfectly with love of God; there always remains room for more. The essence of Catholicism, like its God, is love, calling on us for indefinitely more love.

In its obligation, law is limited; love is unlimited. We can give and receive love only according to our capacity. Since love wants nothing more than more love, it seeks to enlarge its capacity to receive more love by rendering itself more lovable; and it seeks to enlarge its capacity to give love by a greater giving of self.

A small boy was asked what he wished most.

"All the ice-cream I can eat."

"But if you were given that, what then would you wish?"

"A stomach as big as a barrel."

---

[38] *Character of True Devotion,* 84th ed., pp. 85, 86.
[39] *Ibid.,* pp. 56, 57.

A very great good calls for a very great capacity for it. The capacity of creature love to give and to receive love, like the small boy's stomach, is frustratingly small. But our natural love of God, elevated to supernatural love, finds increased capacity to express itself and to receive God's love by becoming more lovable.

"All love is born of love," say St. Augustine, St. Thomas, and St. Bonaventure, as seed is born of seed. The reason is that on earth all good, especially the divine good of grace, is an end which is intended as a means to a greater good. Along with the peace of attainment of the good by the lover, there is developed a greater capacity for good, and a new and greater yearning for it. The good attained is a hostel of rest from which one begins a further and speedier journey to further perfection and transformation of love. Good is not only the end of love; it is the birth of a greater love. It is a form that gives a greater capacity until all possible capacity rests fulfilled in heaven's infinite good.

A small spark in the dry grass by the roadside finds its fuel and then reaches for more, fire changing a whole forest into its own likeness, fuel incorporated into fire which always enlarges its capacity for fuel. Such is love's fuel of finite good — wealth, honor, pleasure — serving only to increase the capacity for more finite good. But the fuel is soon exhausted and is never able to give satisfaction and rest.

Unlike finite good which fails the insatiable capacity of love, God is always there in grace to give Himself more and more to us. As we enlarge our fire of love, we incorporate ourselves more and more into the divine good and He mutually incorporates with us, until we reach in heaven the term of our perfect capacity, perfect satisfaction and perfect beatitude in the fulfillment of our purpose of existence.

9. Reactions to the Challenge of Generosity in Love

A shuffling reaction to love's appeal for generosity is that of some who call themselves realists: "I have no delusions. I'm too modest to aspire to the sanctity of full love. I'm not an eagle living on the peaks of love. I'm only a sparrow. The lowland trees of spiritual life are sufficiently high for me."

Whether or not it is modesty that produces such an attitude, the Sacred Heart has an entirely different idea of His destiny for all of us. St. Paul expresses it: "This is the will of God, your sanctification" (1 Thess. 4:3). Addressed to all, this is a universal vocation to generosity in love of God, to complete union with the will of God in our lives.

In the poem "The Conservative," Charlotte P. Gilman sees

> a black and crimson butterfly a-sitting on a thorn
> . . . all doleful and forelorn.

The writer questions the butterfly: "What can the matter be?" It answers:

> I don't want to be a butterfly; I want to be a worm.
> I don't want to fly; I only want to squirm.

Evolved out of the chrysalis of the law of original sin into Christianity's law of supernatural love, Christians have been given wings of participation in the divinity. We are to fly, not merely to squirm. In love of God we are not meant to be conservative. We belong to the totalitarian right. We are of the Lord's nobility; and we are committed to live in magnanimity befitting our supernatural lineage.

Another reaction to the Sacred Heart's call for wholeness in love is more straightforward: fear: "The slothful man sayeth: There is a lion in the way" (Prov. 26:13). "I'm afraid of the cost involved; it means the cross." To be frank like our Lord, it does mean the cross. We must take up the cross in many small things and in an occasional big one, if we would accept His invitation of love to "come and follow Me." But let us not be unjust to the cross of Christ which our timidity distorts into a crushing load. The fact is that a cross we must bear, either the cross of surrender of our will to Christ, or the far heavier but camouflaged cross consequent to the surrender of will to "the world, the flesh, and the devil." Each and every action of our lives is one or the other surrender, with its cross. There is no neutrality between the two standards as St. Augustine described them: "Love of God to the disregard of self, and love of self to the disregard of God." The sensible as well as the chivalrous choice is evident if we compare the love of the magnanimous Catholic with the life of the chiseling one. We need have no fear of the Master's demand of our whole heart; he wishes only our greatest welfare. We need only to keep hold of His hand — not run ahead of Him by ourselves — and go where He wisely and beneficently leads us.

Fully generous love of God is called upon to give much and often; but it receives much grace to make it possible. It is a question whether the saint, whose abundant grace makes God almost tangible, finds it harder to meet the great demand on his love than the person who is asked for less but with less grace. If we are now only children spiritually, God will not require of us a generosity needing the strength of the spiritual adult. A small child cannot lift a fifty-pound weight, but he can when he grows up. At the prospect of a life of total love we look forward cringingly to the possible sacrifices which may be demanded; but when they are demanded — and they may not be demanded — we shall have grown to the adulthood able to bear them as readily as we bear smaller ones now.

I saw a mother and father taking a Sunday afternoon stroll with their little boy between them holding their hands. When they came to a puddle that had collected in a slight depression of the sidewalk, they said to the child: "Jump!" The little fellow made an effort to jump across the water which, by itself, would have landed it in the puddle; but the parents' hands lifted it over and it toddled along evidently quite proud of its jump. We walk down the street of life holding the hand of our Lord; and when we come to a spiritual puddle, He tells us: "Jump!" and His grace adds the needed strength to our ineffectual effort. We, too, like the child, are apt to continue on our way quite content with our feeble virtue.

Another reaction to the reasonable demand of generosity in love of God is frank and may be cynical: "I'm lazy. I can't raise enough enthusiasm to make the constant effort required." Of course, if one does not pray for grace and meditate on the advantages of a noble love of God, he will not have the needed motivation to live and love generously. This reaction is also irrational. Apart from the fundamental supernatural motives, there is this not insignificant one, which should appeal to the smallhearted. In itself, a life of spiritual effort is psychologically far more pleasant than a life of spiritual sloth, with its attendant dissatisfaction and other unpleasantness.

Love cannot be anything but personal. Christ's love of me calls me by name, as He called Samuel. To so personal a call to love Him, like Samuel we should answer in unreserved generosity: "Speak, Lord, for Thy servant heareth" (1 Kings 3:9). This is no fancy. The stupendous reality is that God alone, by reason of His infinite nature, is personally and wholly interested in each of us. Only the infinite Being can give to each His undivided personal interest. The very state of priesthood is a personal call of our High Priest to a life of total love. A religious is expressly and personally called to seek perfection of love; hence, the religious order is termed "a state tending to perfection." But all human beings, by the fact that they are individually chosen creatures of love, are personally called upon to love wholly the infinite Lovable.

Gratitude is not only a means of expressing our love, as we shall ponder further on; it is also one of the most powerful motives of love of God. Think of your creature dependence on God's love for all that you are, have, and do. Think of His forgiveness of your sins and of His protection of you from other sins that would have ruined you eternally. Think of His personal predilection in His personal graces for you, for His gifts of education and formation, and the sacramental aid of His Mystical Body, the Church. The Sacred Heart tells us: "You have not chosen me, but I have chosen you, and have appointed that you should go and bear fruit" (Jn. 15:16). Do you think, He asks us, that I can be indifferent when you love Me little more than, or not as much as, others who have received only a tithe of the love which I have bestowed on you?

To such positive motivation for generous love of God we can well add the negative and persuasive motive of death — "in a little time our lips are dumb." We have not long to amass the available treasures of love. Christ brings this home to us in His parable of the fig tree. To appreciate its significance we must understand that the vineyard in which the fig tree was planted was protected by guard and even by a wall.

A certain man had a fig-tree planted in his vineyard; and he came seeking fruit thereon, and found none. And he said to the vinedresser: "Behold, for three years now I have come seeking fruit on this fig tree, and I find none. Cut it down, therefore; why does it still encumber the ground?" But he answered him and said: "Sir, let it alone this year too, till I dig around it and manure it" (Lk. 13:6–9).

"One year more" — is that what He tells me? Suppose I were one of the many thousands who yearly hear the diagnosis: inoperable cancer; at most, only one year more. What would I do and not do? Would I not fill my days and hours and minutes with love of God, which alone "you can take with you"? If that is the only reasonable procedure when I have cancer, why is it not peremptory now and always? The rhetoric of death is not merely words but fact. Not to make good use of time to love God is the next thing to the imbecility of making bad use of it, like the pickpocket condemned to death, of whom St. Thomas More says that he "cut the purse" of the judge while passing him to go to prison and to death in a few days.

We must remember too, that "no man is an island." Our lives are interwoven with the lives of others who are better or worse for all eternity because we are better or worse. We are a link in the chain of good worked in the lives of history as intended by God. "A little leaven ferments the whole mass" (Gal. 5:9). If we fail to attain our intended love of God, the "golden chain" of our good influence on our neighbor will be forever missing or diminished. No adult goes to heaven alone. We can enter only by bringing others there by our grace acting through the Mystical Body in the degree of our love of God. Our love of God, the measure of our grace, is the thread on which the pearls of many lives are strung.

II. REASONS FOR LOVING GOD

1. "Who Is Like Unto God"

Psychologists discuss the best way of developing a good habit of will. Some hold that exercise of that habit is essential, since habit is a facility in a kind of act acquired through exercise. Others consider the method of cultivating such a habit to be motivation of the will by the intellect proposing constantly the good attained by the habit. Whatever be the theoretically preferable procedure, we may well join both increased exercise and increased motivation in our quest of quests: the habit of more powerful love of God — supposing, of course, God's grace preceding, accompanying, and completing our meager human efforts to love the All Lovable.

Certainly, intense love of God must have its origin in intense appreciation of Him. Supposing good will, we can love only to the extent that we know the lovable. St. Paul's ardent love and life were prefaced by his mystical appreciation of the person of Christ. His generous: "Lord, what wilt Thou have me to do" was preceded by the answer to his question: "Who art Thou, Lord?" The revelation of His all-inspiring person was Jesus' way of winning to Himself the complete devotion of His enemy Saul. "I am Jesus, whom thou persecutest." We must, with His grace, appreciate Jesus deeply, if we would love Him devotedly and be devotedly His. We must hear Him say, and understand the meaning of His words: "I am Jesus."

Our greatest motive for love of God is complacence that He is what He infinitely is. We love some persons merely because they are what they are, even though we have never seen them, even though they lived long ago, without any reference whatsoever to ourselves as deriving advantage from them. They may be magnanimous, strong, gentle, self-sacrificing, noble, talented, or pleasant:

126

and for that alone we love them. Like God, in His creation, "we see that they are good." This highest and purest of loves, the love of complacence, neither excludes other more self-regarding loves, nor is it necessarily diminished by them. Says St. Francis de Sales:

> Complacence is the great motive of love. It is nothing else . . . than the movement and flowing of the heart to the good, by means of the satisfaction that the good is what it is in itself.[1]

True love leads us fondly to dwell with complacence on the beloved's goodness or worth, with St. Augustine:

> What art Thou, then, my God? . . . Highest, most potent, most omnipotent, most merciful and most just, most hidden and most present. Fairest yet strongest; permanent yet unseizable; changeless yet changing all; never new yet never old. . . . Ever active yet ever at rest; gathering yet needing not; bearing, filling, guarding; creating, nourishing, perfecting; seeking, though nothing is wanting to Thee. What can I say, O God, my Life, my holy joy? Or what can anyone say who speaks of Thee?[2]

Love of God supposes that He is lovable. God must first communicate something lovable to us, in which He then finds complacence, as in an image of His own goodness and worth. Our complacence in God through grace is a participation in God's complacence in Himself. This is properly the esteem of God which intellectual man should evince. The more we love Him, the more we esteem Him; and the more we esteem Him, the more we love Him in greater union of wills.

This love of complacence is "formal" glory to God, what St. Augustine calls "knowledge with praise." God receives perfect, infinite, befitting glory, in which nothing is lacking and which nothing can make greater, in the infinite knowledge and in the consequent infinite esteem and love of His own perfection, which in turn gives rise to His infinite happiness. His inscrutable wisdom has willed to receive the praise, the formal glory of a creation that can intellectually know Him and freely love Him with the love of complacence. This is the heart of the worship of praise.

Relish in God is the very summit of love, to which all the greatest

---

[1] *The Love of God*, 5, 1.
[2] *Confessions*, 1, 4.

lovers of God climb in their ascent of love, and there they habitually abide. It is the most pure love of God for Himself; and in it the soul is most like God and partakes most in God. It is for this love especially that St. Alphonsus Liguori bids us to pray ardently:

> If you wish to acquire the great treasures of the love of God, I recommend that you ask for it continually. . . . Our Lord is liberal in dispensing all His gifts, but particularly in granting the gifts of love to those who ask it; for this love is what He demands of us above all things.[3]

Esteem of God for what He is is the very first step in all love of God and the last destination at which love in its fullness arrives. Without love of complacence, observance of the other commandments is soulless and worthless — "it profiteth nothing." Our interior satisfaction in God must vivify all acts of love or they are not love, but the mere corpse of love. We cannot have the love of desire of God without first esteeming and loving His worth in Himself before we love and esteem His worth for us and for others. So Noldin tells us:

> The commandment of the love of God is not fulfilled merely by the observance of the other (10) commandments; but it must be fulfilled by the act of charity itself. . . . The first and greatest commandment prescribes affective love of God [love of God for Himself].[4]

In God, who gives us participation in Himself as our life in grace, we have all possible motives for the love of complacence and for all other kinds of love; He is infinite lover and infinite lovableness, wisdom, beauty, power, goodness, wealth — all in endless degree.

Think over in your heart all that can attract your love in any and all things and persons: mother, father, spouse, friend. God, ours in grace, is infinite motherliness and infinite fatherliness, infinite spouse and infinite friend. All that mothers and fathers and spouses and friends ever possessed of lovableness, in fact or in our imagination, is in the indwelling God of our grace, but without limit or defect. "Father and mother are kind," says the Danish proverb, "but God is kinder." Christ, our God in grace, who calls us not servants but friends, who is brother to all who do His Father's will,

---

[3] *The True Spouse of Christ*, Ch. 22.
[4] *Theol. Moral.*, n. 340.

Christ our own as our life, is a friend and relative who is the infinite source and sum total of all the dearness of friends and relatives. St. Augustine dwells on this:

> Not with doubtful but with certain consciousness, Lord, I love Thee. Thou hast pierced my heart with Thy word, and I have loved Thee. Both heaven and earth and all that is in them — behold, on all sides they tell me that I should love Thee, nor do they cease to say to all that "they are inexcusable" not to love God. . . .[5]

2. *Only God Can Fill Our Love of Beauty*

> The firmament on high is His beauty, the beauty of heaven with its glorious show (Ecclus. 43:1).

All spiritual beauty of thought that can enchant the mind, all that material nature knows of beauty to show our senses, all that moral beauty can make lovable in fair character is but the hem of the creature garment of God: His beauty's finite reflection. His intrinsic, essential beauty — not which He has, but which He Himself is — is infinite, overwhelmingly incomprehensible to finite eye and spirit, drowning our finite perception, dark because of too much light, incomparably farther beyond our ken and comprehension than the world of scientific thought and formula is beyond the brute's perception. "All that is fair is by nature good." Infinite goodness, God is infinitely fair.

> Cease, then, my tongue and lend unto my mynde
> Leave to bethinke how great that Beautie is,
> Whose utmost parts [visible effects] so beautifull
>   I fynd;
> How much more those essentiall parts [invisible
>   attributes] of His:
> His truth, His love, His wisdom and His blis,
> His grace, His doome, His mercy and His might,
> By which He lends us of Himself a sight.[6]

---

5 *Confessions*, 10, 6, 8.
6 Spenser, "An Hymne of Heavenly Beautie," st. 16.

Bittersweet is the taste of the beauties of earth — sweet for our senses and soul avidly feeding on them, bitter in their aftertaste of sad unsatisfied yearning for transcendental beauty from which they flow and from which we now live in exile. This thirst, says Poe,

> . . . belongs to the immortality of man. . . . It is no mere appreciation of the beauty before us, but a wild effort to reach the beauty above. . . . Inspired by an ecstatic prescience of the glories beyond the grave, we struggle by multiform combinations, among the things and thoughts of time, to attain a portion of that loveliness whose very elements, perhaps appertain to eternity alone.[7]

Beneath the surface of our motion to finite beauty flows the strong current of motion to our destination and of virtual motion to beatitude found in infinite beauty.

If one can regularly get out of the swirling rapids of daily activities and contemplate the many-splendored beauties of life, he perceives with gradually increasing understanding, and with

> A feeling of sadness and longing that is not akin to pain
> And resembles sorrow only as the mist resembles rain
> (Longfellow)

"how much the Lord of them is more beautiful than they" (Wisd. 13:3). This sadness is a child begotten of beauty mated with the human spirit. It is mourning in which we are blessed, for we shall be comforted. Like God and with God through grace, we are like God and with God in loving His beauty as the reason and terminus of our love of the beauty of creatures.

This infinite wellspring of beauty is in our very being through sanctifying grace, a fountain of beauty in us, springing up into eternal beauty — beauty that is not only beloved but also infinite lover, seen now only through the dense haze of finite vision, but soon to be contemplated through participation in that divine beauty's own eyes and mind and heart — beauty itself in all forms and in all attractiveness comprised in a simplicity that never fades on the eye nor palls upon the sense — "beauty ever ancient ever new" — beauty that is all love, and love that is all beauty, for

---

[7] *Works* (New York: Collier, 1903), p. 176.

> The essence of all beauty I call love;
> The attributes, its evidence and end
> (E. B. Browning, *Sword Glare*).

Beauty moves to love; and man's love of beauty is his nostalgia for infinite beauty. Even in its lowest forms of sense-beauty, it wholly engrosses the lives of artists, happy in a life they think well spent, if they can only body it forth in painting, sculpture, or literature. Even in material beauty, how lovable are nature's design and composition, her harmony of color in endless variety, her delicacy and abundance of line and curve, which, in comparison, make the Pitti and the Louvre masterpieces appear the crude scrawl of children.

> O world as God has made it! All is beauty!
> (R. Browning, *Guardian Angel Picture at Fano.*)

Urged by instinct, we are all intent, in varying degree, on the study and reproduction of beauty in our persons and in the environmental setting of our lives. Our love of beauty is our spirit's will for repose in harmony. By the Creator's purpose in grace, we are intended to reproduce finitely in ourselves the divine beauty of the model and maker of all finite beauty. We live with world's beauty as with a courtesan; unless we love her as the daughter of God, it is illicit love.

> We know this Lady Nature.
> This Lady is God's daughter and she lends
> Her hand but to His friends
> But to her Father's friends the hand which thou wouldst win.
> (Francis Thompson, *Nature, Land and Plaint*)

3. *Love of Beauty That Makes the Lover Beautiful*

Material beauty is the "good," or satisfaction, of the eye. Intellectual beauty is the good of the mind. Supernatural beauty is the good of divine man. All beauty, in its degree, tends correspondingly to beautify its contemplator, as medieval Angelus Silesius sings:

> Whate'er thou lovest, Man,
> That too become thou must;
> Christ if thou lovest Christ,
> Dust if thou lovest dust.

Above all is this true of supernatural divine beauty. In grace, we human beings become "other Christs"; beautiful beyond the possibilities of mere men, we "put on Christ" who is beauty itself. "All things are yours," says St. Paul, in the fact that "you are Christ's," who has gathered in Himself as members of His Mystical Body all that is beautiful in heaven and on earth.

St. John of the Cross ardently illuminates Christ as our beauty, in a well-known passage:

> And let us go to see ourselves in Thy Beauty.
>
> Which means: let us so act that, by means of this exercise of love, we may see ourselves in Thy Beauty — that is, that we may be alike in Thy Beauty . . . and that, when either of us looks at the other, each may be like to Thy Beauty and may see himself in Thy Beauty. And thus I shall see Thee in Thy Beauty, and Thou shalt see me in Thy Beauty; and I shall see myself in Thee in Thy Beauty. And so, I may be like to Thee in Thy Beauty and Thou mayest be like to me in Thy Beauty; and my beauty may be Thy Beauty, and Thy Beauty may be my beauty. And I shall be Thou in Thy Beauty, and Thou shalt be I in Thy Beauty, because Thy Beauty Itself will be my beauty.
>
> This is the adoption of the children of God, who will truly say to God that which the Son Himself said to the eternal Father according to St. John: "All that is Mine is Thine; and all that is Thine is Mine" (Jn. 17:10). . . . He, by Essence, being the Son of God by Nature; we, by participation, being children of God by adoption. And thus He spoke, not for Himself, Who is the Head, but for His whole Mystical Body, which is the Church.[8]

God is a mirror, in whom alone we are beautiful, a mirror which does not reflect the beautiful outside itself, but makes beautiful all and only that which is reflected in it. God is love that makes the lover lovable. God must love me before I am worth loving.

It is the beautiful that we love; but it is love that is beautifying. Hence, after the inspired Word, the Councils and Fathers of the

---

[8] *Spiritual Canticle* 36, 5; *Vida y obras de San Juan de la Cruz*, ed. R. P. Licinio, O.C.D., Madrid, 1955, p. 1089.

Church associate most intimately the virtue of love and beautify-ing grace. Thus St. Augustine, with characteristic ardor, comments on the words of St. John's Epistle (1:4, 19), "Let us love God because He hath loved us first":

> Our soul, my brethren, is ugly through iniquity; by loving God it is made beautiful. What kind of love is that which renders the one loving beautiful? God is always beautiful, never defective, never changeable. He loved us first, because He is always beauti-ful; and whom did He love except the ugly and deformed? Not however, in such a way that He would let them go away ugly, but that He would change them and from deformed render them beautiful. As your love increases, so increases your beauty; for love is the soul's beauty.[9]

As the Father's enveloping love goes all out to the Son in whom He contemplates His own individual and identical beauty, so the Son's enveloping love goes out to all of us, His brothers and sisters, made so in the degree of our grace by which His own beauty is shared in us. His heart rejoices in His reflection in us: "Behold, thou art fair, my beloved, and comely" (Cant. 1:15). Our purpose of life is the quest of beauty; we are to be "rich men in virtue, studying beauty" (Ecclus. 44:6), that the Lord may bless us with the beauty of justice (cf. Jer. 31:23).

4. Love as Gratitude

Gratitude must have a large part in all love, but especially in love of God. Gratitude is delicate love. Gratitude, "the memory of the heart," is a dear duty, and in the last analysis always a religious duty, whether it be directly to God or indirectly to our fellows, whether it be for temporal or for spiritual benefits, whether it be for joy or suffering. So St. Paul bids us (1 Thess. 5:18): "In all things give thanks"; for all that happens to us is from the hand of God, and from the hand of an infinitely good and loving God can come only good and love. God cannot act except in an act of love and

---

[9] *In ep. Joan.* tr. 9, n. 9; *PL* 35, 2051.

God wills and acts in all that happens to us. This is as true as God is. God *is* substantial love itself.

Dwell on our being loved by One on whom from moment to moment depends not only all that we have but also the fact that at any moment we are. It is not fitting that we disregard the individual and minutely constant attention and solicitude of God for us — indispensable, not only in order to act, but even in order fundamentally to exist. We should, at least at times, receive on our knees in gratitude all that we are and do. "Lambs," according to the Chinese proverb, "have the grace to suck kneeling." God's will is God's love. Creation is no other activity than the loving and willing of God. He does not need nor use instruments. His love penetrates to the taproot of being of all creatures, as to *what* they are, as to *that* they are, as to *why* they are. God's love is the operation of His infinite nature, the reason for all.

Some imagine that God acts through creatures which mediate His action on other creatures. So thought Plato and other Greek philosophers, in their belief that God acted only on the highest ninth heaven, as Dante tells us, and that this ninth heaven transmitted the action through the eight other concentric heavens down to creatures of earth. Only on a secondary, collateral, and finite level, the creature does its action and has its effect. On the primary creative level, God eminently does all creature action and effect, inasmuch as it is a positive entity. God operates immediately in all creature being and action. His will activity, or love, has neither any intervening cause nor any intervening action affecting the being and action of any creature. The influence of any creature A on any creature B is infinitely more God's influence on creature B. In every possible way, His love or will is cause of all creature effect, the cause of every creature cause, and the cause of every creature action. Not only in our beginning but at every moment, we and our action are the choice of the will and love of God, except as to our freely chosen negation of order in our action, which is sin, and of which we are the sole cause.

None of us, none of our actions are lost to God, in the multitude of human persons and human actions. God's will, God's love, gives personal and individual attention to each of us, constantly and carefully pouring existence into each of us from moment to moment. We and all creatures, at every instant, are products of God's love in our favor. The only congruous response to such individual loving attention of our Creator is our frequent grateful attention to Him. This sense of mandatory return of love as gratitude is the motivation of the anxious cry of Saul converted into Paul: "Lord, what wilt thou have me do?" (Acts. 9:6.) It is the cry of all noble souls first aware of their obligation of gratitude in the face of all that God has done for them. It is the cry of the soul receiving its God in Mass: "What shall I return to Thee for all that Thou hast given to me?"

The poet is entranced by his vision of the beauty of earth and sky. The saint is in ecstasy contemplating, in the beauty of creation, its infinite source, beauty itself. Loyola tells us that

> It was for him supreme consolation to gaze on the midnight sky and its stars, which he did often and for long periods, since in doing so he felt a powerful urge to serve our Lord.[10]

This sense of grateful wonder for the God of nature seen in His creatures remained with Ignatius all his life. It was similar to the better known gratitude of St. Francis of Assisi. It is the proper spirit of man.

Hugh of St. Victor (1096–1141) was the leader of the school of the Victorines in the monastery of St. Victor in Paris. He was a theologian of dominating influence in the twelfth century, developing scholasticism in its cradle. He opens the same approach to love of God in his *Earnest of the Soul* as does St. Ignatius in his *Contemplation of Divine Love* in the *Exercises,* namely the deep channel of gratitude:

> I confess to Thee, my Lord, my God, Thy great mercies to me: that Thou didst not abandon me, O savior of my life and light of my eyes. "What shall I render to Thee for all that Thou hast given me?" (Ps. 115.) Thou wishest that I love Thee. And how shall I love Thee? and nevertheless, I shall love Thee, my Lord, my Strength, my Foundation, my Refuge, my Liberator, my God, my Helper, my Protector, the Horn of my salvation, my Re-

---

10 MHSJ. Narr. I, 376, 11.

ceiver, and what else may I say? "Thou art the Lord, my God"
(Ps. 17).

Thou hast given me to learn of Thee; and out of many others,
to know the revelations of Thy secrets [of Christianity]. . . . Thou
hast given more truly to know Thee, more purely to love Thee,
more sincerely to believe in Thee, more ardently to follow Thee
. . . and often, when I seemed to be consumed, suddenly Thou
hast liberated me. When I wandered, Thou hast led me back.
When I was ignorant, Thou hast taught me. When I was sad,
Thou didst console me. When I despaired, Thou didst strengthen
me. When I fell, Thou didst raise me. When I went, Thou didst
lead me. When I came, Thou didst receive me. . . .[11]

Hugh is echoing the psalmist David, who wrote his doubly inspired poems largely as reasons inspired by God for grateful love.

Thou hast held me by thy right hand; and by thy will thou hast
conducted me . . . for what have I in heaven, and besides thee
what do I desire on earth? For thee my flesh and my heart hath
fainted away: thou art the God of my heart, and the God that is
my portion forever (Ps. 72:24–26).

Regret for sin, repentance, expiation for one's own and for the
ingratitude of others to God, are but the negative expression of
gratitude, "the exchequer of the poor," as Shakespeare calls it, paying our debts. While man rejects God, God continues to love him
creatively. He does not totally reject him but paternally makes it
possible for him to regain his lost supernatural being, being for
which he was made and without which is absolute frustration.

Penitent love is a necessary part of gratitude by which we who
have sinned against love must make reparation to God who is love.
St. Augustine gives beautiful witness to his own ardent penitent love:

Too late have I loved Thee, O Beauty ever ancient, ever new!
Too late have I loved Thee; and behold, Thou wert within me
and I was outside; and there I was seeking Thee. And ugly, I
rushed into those beautiful creatures. Thou wert within me, and
I was not with Thee. Those things kept me afar from Thee, which,
if they were not in Thee, they would not be. Thou didst call me
and cry aloud through my deafness. Though didst blaze forth;
Thou wert brilliant; and Thou didst dispel my blindness. Thou
didst exhale Thy fragrance and I drew breath; and I panted for

---

[11] *PL* 176, 954.

Thee; and I trusted Thee; and I have hungered and thirsted for Thee. Thou didst touch me, and I was inflamed with Thy peace. . . .[12]

In the early development of telephone communication, at times a mouse with a thread attached to it was sent through a narrow conduit. The thread was tied to a strong twine, and the twine to a small cable which pulled a coaxial cable through the conduit, thus establishing many lines of communication. Gilbert K. Chesterton tells us that before his conversion to Catholicism his tenuous relation with God was by "one thin thread of thanks." Gratitude is love; and such a thread, though small, is the means of drawing into the soul a coaxial cable of supernatural union, with multivaried communication with God.

5. God's Quest of Our Love

Nothing will start a fire as readily as another fire. Nothing will start a love as readily as another love. Love is electric in its strength of attraction for love. But superior love, seeking love from the greatly inferior, is fairly irresistible. The eloquent Dominican, Lacordaire, declares:

> Love has one essential need from which it cannot free itself, namely, to be loved. Love forgives everything except one thing; and that is, not to be loved. . . . God pursues mankind, soul by soul, day by day, and it is only when He is rejected and contemned at the last hour of our life, that He takes back His love and abandons us forever.[13]

"I have loved thee with an everlasting love" (Jer. 31:3). The love of God carried me, from all eternity, in the womb of His mind. His love gave supernatural as well as natural birth to me. His parental love fostered, protected, and educated me; and the exultation of my love should burst forth from my heart, as it burst forth from the heart of St. Claire of Jesus: "My God loves *me!*" (Italics hers.)

---

12 *Confessions,* 10, 27, 38; *PL* 32, 795.
13 *Conference* 72, 1851.

The same generous reaction to God's love was that of St. Francis de Sales:

> I will never depart from Him. I will die with Him, consumed in the flames of His love. The same fire of love shall consume the divine Creator and His poor creature.[14]

Mystical St. Bernard, the "mellifluent doctor," is similarly swept up in the chariot of God's love for us:

> [Christ's love of us in His Passion] in every way clearly demands our whole love for Him. This, I say, is that which so gently persuades our devotion and so justly demands it, and so intimately constrains it, and so vehemently moves its feeling.[15]

Divine is the pathos and divine the sublimity of that candid word-photograph of the Savior (Jn. 7:37–39): "Jesus stood and cried out: 'If anyone thirst, let him come to me and drink.'" We can well imagine Christ saying of His nonhuman creation:

> But what are these things to me?
> They lack not me; they are full-planned;
> I must have love in my degree
> A human heart, a human hand.
>   (Dixon, *The Wanderer*)

God wished to create, not only beings loved by Him, but also beings who are lovers of Him. Incredible is the tenderness of God's longing for the love of His creatures to whom He communicates His Holy Spirit to love Him in their loves. He has inspired the authors of Holy Writ, in many places, to express His yearning to be loved.

> Today if you shall hear his voice, harden not your hearts (Ps. 94:8).

> All the day long I stretched out my hand to a people unbelieving and contradicting (Rom. 10:21).

> Do not grieve the Holy Spirit of God (Eph. 4:30).

"He who loves me will be loved by my Father, and I will love him and will manifest myself to him" (Jn. 14:21); such is Christ's offer, His divine love for our creature love. "Charity makes gods out of

---

14 *On the Love of God*, trans. H. B. Mackey, 1953, p. 555.
15 *In Cantic.* 20, 2; *PL* 183, 867.

men," says St. Maximus.[16] Christ our God, ineffably loving the creature of His mere wish, strains His omnipotence to make Himself
our brother, not only in His humanity which in itself is unbelievable
condescension, but even in His divinity. He desires that we love
Him, not merely with our faint human love, but even with His
divine love in which we are participants. He forestalls our love
with His necessary grace and then He meets our love with His
far more than answering love.

"There is no greater invitation to love," says St. Augustine, "than
the love of God for us which has forestalled our love."[17] St. Prosper
under Augustine's influence repeats his master's idea: "Man has been
inspired with love by God who has loved man first, when man did
not love God."[18] And it seems the ultimate in understatement that,
as St. Caesarius says, "No one has loved us more than God has
loved us."[19] In the same way that Augustine speaks of grace as our
holiness, he speaks of grace as our charity: "The charity of God
is poured forth in our hearts (Rom. 5:5), not only that charity by
which God has loved us, but also that by which He made us to
love Him."[20] Of course, St. Augustine's assertion: "The love, which
is from God and is God, is properly the Holy Spirit,"[21] must be
understood as not excluding the other two persons; for he says that
the three persons collaborate in the gift of charity, and that we
must love all three, and we must love through all three.

Christ bids us to "abide in His love," loved and loving, His ocean
of love engulfing and absorbing our thimbleful of creature love: "As
the Father hath loved me, I also have loved you. Abide in my love"
(Jn. 15:9). It is of this love of God for us that Origen says: "If we
can love God it is because God loves us."[22]

Christ, eager that we be entirely His in love, asks in the words of
the Canticle (8:6): "Put me as a seal upon thy heart, as a seal upon
thy arm." He wishes to keep our heart's affections sealed as His
property. He seeks always to be loved in all our loves of other persons and things. He desires that the feelings of our heart toward

---

16 *Epist. 2 ad Joan. cubic.*
17 *De catech. rud.* 4, 7; *PL* 40, 314.
18 *In 1 Joan.* 10, 10; *PL* 35, 2052.
19 *Serm.* 38, 3; *PL* 44, 237.

20 *De Spirit. et Lit.* 32; *PL* 44, 231.
21 *In Joan.* tr. 102, 5; *PL* 35, 1898.
22 *In Rom.* 4:9; *PG* 14, 997.

persons and events be such that they can be His own feelings. He asks that all the works of our arm, throughout our daily activities, be sealed with His activity and glory in them, all done in Him, all done for Him, all done according to His will, so that the love of God is the motive of every feeling and every action of our life. Loving us, He wishes to be sole owner and complete master of us in every way.

Hence Father Willie Doyle, S.J., tells us:

> "The truest title to address our divine Lord by, is 'Poor Jesus.' He is rich in all (earth's) things except the one he really cares about: the love of our loving hearts."

God of our grace made Himself our Father, not only by inspiring into us human life and soul, but even by drawing us into that eternal stream of divine nature and life flowing from Him and constituting His Son — all that we may be His divinely loving children. Not merely a human heart is given us with which to love God; He so desires our love that He gives us participation in the Heart of His Son to love Him with: "the Holy Spirit . . . has been given to us" (Rom. 5:5).

If a heart exists, every other heart — first of all, the divine Heart — wants the love of that heart. "In this is the love, not that we have loved God, but that He has first loved us" (1 Jn. 4:10). Not only is the love of God the source of the supernatural lovableness of our being, through sanctifying grace; He is also, through actual grace, the stimulant and source of our every act of love of Him.

6. Christ Pleads for Our Love

God's quest of man's love brought Him as Christ to win back mankind's love as a whole; and He is eager to come to each individual person and regain him or her to His love. He entreats each of us to return to His love, in His repeated entreaty to Israel expressed through Jeremias:

Thou hast prostituted thyself to many lovers: nevertheless return to me, saith the Lord, and I will receive thee (3:1).

Return, O rebellious Israel, saith the Lord, and I will not turn away my face from you (3:12).

Return, you rebellious children; and I will heal your rebellions (3:22).

If thou wilt return, O Israel, saith the Lord, return to me (4:1).

In order that He may induce us to love Him, who at any instant could wish into existence countless myriads far more lovable than we are, our Creator argues the merits of His plea for our love. Infinite, self-sufficient Master, He presses us to consider how absolutely necessary He and love of Him are for our happiness and welfare. To bring home to our hearts, so "slow to understand," how desperately we need Him and how eagerly we should seek union with Him, He describes Himself by metaphors taken from things most fundamentally necessary for our existence and well-being; He presses His claim to our love by ardently emphasizing what He is for us and what He will do for us if we love Him in return.

He would deepen our love and thought of Him for what He is to us, not as though He were something outside us, but precisely as our indwelling God of grace, associated with us, one with us as very life, transfusing our nature and person into His, merging our puny powers to know, love, and possess Him with a participation in His divine powers of glorifying and possessing Himself.

I am the vine, you are the branches. He who abides in me, and I in him, he bears much fruit; for without me you can do nothing (Jn. 15:5). Abide in me, and I in you (ibid. 4).

I am the good shepherd, and I know mine and mine know me. . . . I lay down my life for my sheep (Jn. 10:14, 16).

I am the door of the sheep. . . . If anyone enter by me he shall be safe, and shall go in and out, and shall find pastures (ibid. 10:7–10).

I have come a light into the world, that whoever believes in me may not remain in the darkness (ibid. 12:46).

I came that they may have life, and have it more abundantly (ibid. 10:10).

These things I have spoken to you that in me you may have peace (ibid. 16:33).

Peace I leave with you, my peace I give to you; not as the world gives do I give to you (*ibid.* 14:27).

Consider again, He asks: What shall I be to you?

I appoint to you a kingdom, even as my Father has appointed to me, that you may eat and drink at my table in my kingdom (Lk. 22:29, 30).

I give them (my sheep) everlasting life and they shall never perish, neither shall anyone snatch them out of my hand (Jn. 10:28, 29).

He who believes in me, even if he die, shall live (*ibid.* 11:25).

Whoever lives and believes in me, shall never die (*ibid.* 11:26).

As I live because of the Father, so he who eats me, he also shall live because of me. . . . He who eats this bread shall live forever (*ibid.* 6:58, 59).

He who eats my flesh, and drinks my blood, abides in me and I in him (*ibid.* 6:57).

Amen, amen, I say unto you, unless you eat the flesh of the Son of Man, and drink his blood, you shall not have life in you (*ibid.* 6:54).

The bread that I will give is my flesh for the life of the world (*ibid.* 6:52).

He who drinks of the water that I will give shall never thirst (*ibid.* 4–13).

He who believes in me, as the Scripture say, "From within him there shall flow rivers of living water" (*ibid.* 7:38).

Come to me, all you who labor and are burdened, and I will give you rest (Mt. 11:28).

Christ as our human brother is our power with the divine throne; and His intercession, not only for us but also in us, is infallible in its fulfillment. In fact, He directs us to speak in His name, and we shall receive all that we ask: "Amen, amen, I say to you, if you ask the Father anything in my name, he will give it to you" (Jn. 16:23–24). Hence St. Augustine urges us:

When God says to thee: "Ask what thou wilt," what are you going to ask? Rouse thy mind; excite thy greed; push to the utmost and dilate thy desire. It is no ordinary person, but God Himself, who has said: "Ask what thou wilt." . . . Still thou wilt find nothing dearer, nothing better than Him who has made all. Ask Him for Himself; and in Him and from Him, thou shalt have all things that He has made.[23]

7. God's Love of Us Is Personal

God's love is not a collective love, in which we are loved as a group but not as individuals. His love is not like the president's love for Americans, whom he loves as a nation but does not know and love individually. God not only loves us with a personal love, but He also loves us as though each of us were the only existing creature. Hence, Newman observes:

> God beholds thee individually, whoever thou art. "He calls thee by name." He sees thee and understands thee. He knows what is in thee, all thy own particular feelings and thoughts, thy disposi-tions and likings, thy strength and thy weakness. He views thee in thy day of rejoicing and in thy day of sorrow. He sympathizes in thy hopes and in thy temptations; He interests Himself in all thy anxieties and in thy remembrance, and in all the risings and fallings of thy spirit. He compasses thee round and bears thee in His arms; He takes thee up and sets thee down. Thou dost not love thyself better than He loves thee. Thou canst not shrink from pain more than He dislikes thy bearing it; and if He puts it on thee, it is as thou wilt put it on thyself, if thou art wise, for a greater good afterward.[24]

The human person rises, through the possessiveness of love, to the greatest perfection in possession of another. The beloved is reproduced in the mind of the lover, and thus is internally possessed. Says the wise à Kempis:

> For many a time I am not there where I am bodily standing or sitting, but I am rather where my thoughts carry me. There am I where my thought is; and there oftentimes are my thoughts where that which I love is.[25]

But the innermost sanctuary of all personal possession is attained through union of wills, which is called generally union of hearts.

---

23 *Enarr. in Ps.* 34.
24 *Parochial and Plain Sermons* V, 124–125.
25 *The Following of Christ,* Bk. 4, c. 48.

This is the most intense and intimate possession of a human being. It is spiritual oneness of our will with the will of the beloved, in the satisfaction that he is what he is and we wish everything good for him.

This unitive possession through union of thought and will is the worth that we cherish in true love; for all other modes of possession and union are impersonal, external, and material. No treasure on earth is greater than the wealth of possessing another human being's benevolent thought and of being possessed in it. All other expressions of love are merely the robes of love, which, without union of mind and heart, are tawdry sham, while possession of the heart alone suffices. This is what we mean by personal union with God: union and participation of His mind and will in our mind and will; and God's mind and will, being infinite, constitute a union with us which on His part is infinitely personal.

Among creatures, to love some is to omit others from our love. Yet to love God is to love everything else, because all else that is worth loving is seen in Him, and He is seen in all else. In God's loving, all the irreducible antinomies of love are reconciled: absolutely intense and total love, the greatest possible love of all else and infinite love bestowed on each one, and yet on all of us.

Man is a person to God; other creatures of earth are merely numbers. By man's participation in God's essence through grace, the Creator's personal providence for man becomes the personal attitude of a father toward His adopted child and of a brother toward an adopted fellow child. This total love is of an intensity which perceives in us, not merely an image of Himself, but Himself indwelling in us in His very reality, our life merged into His life while remaining our life, His own natural Son constituting us His adopted but real divine children in grace. His eye rests on us with a complacence born of the infinite complacence found in His own infinite goodness.

The human mind and heart have always had a strong attraction for unification with the divine source of all; but often this attraction has led intellectuals into barren and self-contradictory pantheism and monism, in which God is degraded below our level as impersonal nature. In the true pantheism taught by our Lord and realized through Him we have the full satisfaction of our longing for personal union with absolute being, worth, and loveliness — not a mere sterile idea for dissection by philosophers, but a living, personal, intelligent, and loving union with the infinite being of the creator and source of all good.

Coming "from God who is our home," we children of the infinite are placed in this orphan asylum of the world; and we feel our hearts, attracted as they may be to finite goods of our environment, filled with unsatisfied nostalgia for our infinite parent for whom we are made. The Sermon on the Mount, in its Beatitudes, is full of divine answers to the yearnings of our divinized beings: "for they shall be filled," "for they shall see God."

How intimately He wills to be transfused into us in love-possession is fervently shown in His chosen symbol of that union: our nutrition. Under it He seeks expression of the inexpressible intimacy of supernatural fusion of our life into His life, a union which His possessiveness asks and even commands: "Amen, Amen, I say unto you, unless you eat the flesh of the Son of Man and drink his blood, you shall not have life in you" (Jn. 6:54).

Security in possession of the beloved is the engrossing concern of personal love. The inevitable and definite frustration of all loves of earth shall not frustrate him who abides in Christ's love. Since we participate in His eternal life we participate in the consoling security of His everlasting love, a security of which He explicitly assures us:

> I give them everlasting life; and they shall never perish; neither shall anyone snatch them out of my hand. What my Father has given me is greater than all; and no one is able to snatch anything out of the hand of my Father. I and the Father are one (Jn. 10:28–30).

8. Possession Undivided

Love is fulfilled in possession; and as far as the divine is above created nature, so far is grace's supernatural possession of God by us, and of us by God, above all possible possession by mere natural creature love. Spouse of the soul, God in ineffable condescension wishes to share His goods with us. In grace, we participate even in His divine manner of loving.[26]

"The love of God demands the whole of you, since it made you," Augustine reminds us.[27] On His part, He gives us through grace participation in His own divine powers of possessing Himself, in the attitude of the Song of Songs: "My beloved to me, and I to him" (Cant. 2:16).

False love, like Carmen, always demands that we sacrifice true love to it; then it abandons us after our painful rejection of true love, leaving us totally without love. Love of God demands that we give up, painfully, all false loves; but it will not abandon us until we abandon it; and it contains in itself infinitely all that any and all creature love can contain.

Why is God so insistent on being loved, as both the Old and New Testaments give testimony? Because in possessing the love of the creature He possesses the willing creature, as He should, in perfect degree. He has given man a free heart with which to love in order that, in his love, man might freely give back to God what is His own. When the lover says to the beloved: I am thine, he expresses the state of a possessed being, into which love has brought him. And if the beloved loves the lover, both have come into the state of the greatest possible mutual possession. St. Francis de Sales emphasizes this possession through love:

> We are more in God than in ourselves; we live more in Him than in ourselves. We are in such sort from Him, by Him, for Him and belonging to Him, that we cannot intently consider what we are to Him and what He is to us, without being forced to exclaim: I am thine, Lord, since I have my being *from* Thee. I must love Thee as my purpose and center of existence, since I am *for* Thee. I must love Thee more than my own being, since my being subsists *through* Thee. I must love Thee more than myself, since I am wholly Thine and *in* Thee (italics mine).[28]

---

[26] Cf. St. John of the Cross, p. 148.
[27] *Serm.* 34:7.
[28] *On the Love of God*, tr. H. B. Mackey, p. 438 f.

Free in choice and in our loves, we possess ourselves, we own ourselves, we are personal, in the highest creature degree. Love of God is sublime on our side precisely because we give ourselves to God as no nonfree creature can; and on the side of God our love is the possession of the free God who meets our free choice of Him with His free choice of us.

God is not only the sole all-inclusive lovable; He is also the sole undivided love. We find in Him a love for us that we all seek but seek absolutely in vain outside of Him. Our very nature makes us deficiently lovable and deficient lovers. We cannot find a creature to love us with an undivided love, not because human love is too great to be undivided, but because it is too small. The smaller the love is, the more it is frustratingly divided. The infinite love cannot be divided. In God alone, we can find total love for us and in Him alone we can find total lovableness. Our Lord tells St. Catherine of her happy state and that of other souls like her:

> How glorious is that soul which has been really able to leave the stormy ocean and come to Me, the Sea Pacific, and in that sea, which is Myself, to fill the pitcher of her heart.[29]

God's love, dwelling in us, both naturally and supernaturally diffuses Him and His uncreated will into the very roots of our being and will. Christ's love is the gift and transmission of Himself into us as our very life. We can say to Him: "Thou, kind fellow, gavest thyself away gratis; and I thank thee for thee."[30]

When the millionaire gives his wife a costly chinchilla coat, how much of a gift does she see in it? As much as she finds his love in it. The wife of an unskilled laborer may find his gift of a cheap coat far greater, in which she feels clothed in his love for her.

To will only what the beloved God wills, to live and act only as He wills, to accept all that He wills concerning our person — such a fusion of wills is the only and supreme way of diffusing ourselves, as it were, into our beloved God. This is to give oneself totally to the beloved, a donation imperative in complete love.

---

[29] *Dialogues*, 89.
[30] *2 Henry IV*, 4, 3, 74.

In all finite love there is an abyss of externality between the loving and the loved which is utterly unbridgeable. No creature was made to possess another creature or to be possessed by it completely and exclusively as its own. In human love, there is hopeless impossibility of that fusion of being, that permeating fusion, which is the ideal of the avid possessiveness of love and toward which it ardently strains. That transcendent possession is reserved for the exclusive owner of creatures and of creatures' love. Finite love is doomed to thwarting indirectness and to painful restriction by the nature of the loving possessor and of the loved one possessed.

Complete dedication of self to the beloved in human loves is the longed-for ideal; but it is impossible, and an attempt to live it has only the outcome of either disillusionment or death. Romancers, consequently, end their love stories with the death of the lovers rather than leave them in the practical frustrations which absolute love entails in daily human life. Unlike all creature love, which is necessarily anxious and thwarted in its limitations, love of God in grace, with its total absorption of our persons and lives by God, adapts us to the interior and exterior peace of total fulfillment. Nor is it strange. The very purpose of man's nature is the domination of love of God over all his other loves.

Fulfilled love is not only possession of the beloved, but a possession that would find all in the beloved, nor look for other goods that are not in the beloved. For that reason, all creature love of creature is fated to be foiled. No creature beloved has anything like all the good that can be loved. No love can be sated in creatures, and therefore no creature can be loved exclusively. God alone is the worthy object and the fulfillment of that boundless potentiality of love; and if there is anything that can be loved outside of Him, it must be a reason for loving Him the more.

Outside of God we need not go to find anything lovable; and all that we find lovable outside Him is infinitely more lovable in Him. He asks: If you love wealth, why do you love merely the clay creature? In your love of the creature, why do you not love Me, the endless realm of Gold? If you love beauty, why do you love only created beauty which is far more defective than it is perfect, while you do not love Me who am Beauty without bound? If you love knowledge of created facts, why do you not love Me the word, infinite Wisdom itself, and cause of all creature fact? If you love love, why do you love a creature that loves, and do not love Me who not only love infinitely but am also all possible love unlimited?

9. Love Incomprehensible

Love brings about a sort of equalization of the lovers which is often called fellowship. "Friendship," says St. Thomas, "is based on some fellowship of life; for nothing is so proper to friendship as to live together."[31] Hence, Aristotle says correctly, from the viewpoint of reason alone — but falsely in our knowledge of the revelation of grace — that "when the gap is very wide, as between men and God, friendship is no longer possible." Divine Love, the Holy Spirit, raises man in grace to adoptive fellowship in the divinity; and we live together in Christ in supernatural intimacy, our very life in His very life.

Love may be measured by that which we are ready to give the beloved, through all the values of things until it arrives at total love which is the unreserved giving of self. This is God's unimaginable love of His creature man: the gift of Himself in grace, in which He asks: "What is there that I ought to do more to my vineyard, that I have not done to it?" (Isa. 5:4.)

The greatest objection to faith in the Incarnation of God is the infinite God's love for finite man, which, as St. Paul says, "emptied," as it were, the divinity of itself and "took on the form of a slave," which for God is next to nothingness. Were it not a known fact of revelation, we could not conceive the all-sufficient God as manifesting such a love for such a nothing as the creature is. When St. Bridget asked our Lord: "Lord, why have You chosen me, who am so worthless?" Jesus made answer: "Sometimes I choose to drink from golden cups, sometimes from silver ones; now I choose to drink from a wooden one. Thus I have chosen thee."

---

[31] *Summa*, 2-2, 25, 3.

> Whom wilt thou find to love ignoble thee?
> Save Me, save only Me?
> > (*The Hound of Heaven*)

The engulfing humility of the tragic character that was Francis Thompson is proper to all of us. The pathos of our lowliness before God is aptly figured in the first meeting of the pitiable poet and drug addict with Meynell, as described by Meynell's daughter in her book, *Francis Thompson and Wilfred Meynell*.

> My father, being in his workroom, was told that Mr. Thompson wished to see him. "Show him up," he said and was left alone. Then the door opened and a strange hand was thrust in. The door closed, but Thompson had not entered. Again it opened and again it shut. At a third attempt, a waif of a man came in. No such figure had been looked for; more ragged and unkempt than the average beggar, with no shirt beneath his coat and bare feet in broken shoes, he found my father at a loss for words.

Thompson speaks of his feelings in that situation:

> At Fate's dread portal then
> Even so stood I, I ken,
> Even so stood I, between a joy and fear (*Sister Song*).

"We have come to know, and have believed, the love that God has in our behalf" (1 Jn. 4:16). Christianity is the intensest possible love; and when we have it, it "casteth out fear" of any other loss (*ibid.* 18). Our religion is filial confidence in the security of being "in Christ," the adopted divine child of God who loves us incomprehensibly.

10.   All Law Is Love

From time to time, the Church emphasizes in her writers and saints the doctrine of love of God as a law for her children. It was announced by the Moses of Christianity, Christ, in His two commandments as the résumé of the ten commandments. A pity it is, that many of the Church's children persist in looking on God as a ubiquitous and omniscient policeman waiting to punish us, rather than as a benevolent father guiding us, solicitous for our welfare.

The Fathers, after St. Paul, inspired the first Christians to "aim at charity (love)" (1 Cor. 14:1). It is not strange, then, that the great classics in moral theology have all proposed love of God as the law of living. Of late, another swell of thought and feeling of love as law has been sweeping over the ocean of Catholicity.[32]

However, the principle of love as law is not exclusively the specific principle of revealed law, theology. It is also the basic principle of the law of reason, called ethics, which Christ assumed, simplified, and supernaturalized as His law for all human living, personal and social. Love is the purpose of each human action and the norm and obligation of human existence as a whole. For this reason, the penetrating mind of Aquinas could not fail to lay down the ethical principle of reason, which is supernaturalized in grace as the principle of Christianity: "No strictly true virtue is possible without love of God."[33] "Moral virtues," he says,[34] "which make a man good, are directed to their ultimate end," God, through love.

A life of law, obedience, authority, and obligation is not, in itself, opposed to a life of love. Human sense perception is not opposed to, but transfused by, intellectual perception. So obligation and obedience are transfused by love of God.

The Old Testament was not a law bereft of love as some seem unwisely to propose it. In the New Testament love is in the law in greater degree; and of course is supernaturalized. But obedience to law without love of God is no virtue of obedience. Pascal's objection to God viewed as "embodied law" was unjustified. Law, which is order, is born and lives in the love begetting it — love of eternal order, which is reflected as God's extrinsic glory in its child, the natural order, and in its grandchild, positive, or freely chosen, order of society. God's law, the source of all law, both objectively and subjectively is love; and God's love is not merely a powerful, beautiful, and beneficent law; it is the power, beauty, and beneficence of all law. Take life out of the most handsome and powerful physique and

---

32 Cf. *Theology Digest*, Vol. 2, 1, 1954, pp. 15–25.
33 *Summa*, 2–2, 23, 7, c.
34 *Ibid.* 3.

faculties and they are nullified and worthless. Take love of God out
of any noble and wise law and it is like a human body without
a soul.

Plato seems to have held that there is "eros," or love, as a vital
principle of all things and action: a love of order, or better, a love
which is order. How far he personified this principle, eros, is not
plain. While we hold this Platonic principle of love as really law,
we hold that there is also a personal love, God's will and nature, as
the source of law. Law is love. Man is moral in freely aligning
himself with this eros which is God's will. Ethics is the science and
the practice of love.

Starting from God's love for creatures, which is creation, we find
that the purpose of creatures is to return love for their Creator, as
His extrinsic glory, in their reflection of His infinite perfection. All
law of God for His creatures is His love seeking their good by which
He is glorified; and all our observance of His law is our corresponding
love for God. Thus ethical law is reduced to the simple and absolute
norm and obligation of love of God in our actions, which is nothing
else than union of our will and nature with God's will and nature
by following the laws of our nature which He gave us. God intended all mankind to live morally. Hence He gave this easily understood guide and responsibility of love in union of will with His
will, which is intelligible to any normal mind. To all it is apparent
that if He gave us this human nature with its laws, He intended us
to perfect it as His glory, by observing those laws. Thus love of
God is the law of ethics with a minimum of metaphysics. By it, the
majority of mankind are moral and holy. "The purpose of this
charge (the law) is love" (1 Tim. 1:5).

The law of love is the law in all laws, the *lex legum*. Love is the
center whose radii extend to the whole circumference of laws. In
observing this law we virtually observe all law. "They that love
Him [the Lord], shall be filled with His law" (Ecclus: 2:19). The
beauty of the house of creation is its order expressing the law of
God's love. The essence of sin is disorder. Love not only makes all
order, it also reorders all disorder. Whatever law has been trans-
gressed by man is restored to observance by this one law of love. It
is the "act of perfect contrition" for all transgression. Of this law

the psalmist speaks when he teaches (1:2): "Blessed is the man . . . whose will [love] is in the law of the Lord."

Just as there is no law and no personal virtue which, as St. Thomas teaches, is not love of God, so there is no social virtue or social law which is not love of neighbor, and therefore love of God. All valid law of human governors is an expression of God's love of man, whom He made social so that he could be perfected in his life by the law of the State, even though the human lawmaker has no such idea of God. All valid social law, whether of parents or of the State, all spiritual law, whether of our nature as ethics or of Christ and His Church as supernatural law — law of any kind — should be viewed as God's love of us and of our welfare, which is met by our love of God in our obedience to the law.

There is crying need of this view of law among juveniles as regards their parents and citizens as regards their State, rather than for them to see law, as the majority do, only as subjection to other human wills. Because a majority of Americans do not relate right and wrong action with love of God, we have become, as sociologists tell us, the most lawless people of the world, without the excuse of poverty that some other nations proffer.

There can be no obedience to human law which is not, at least virtually, love of the over-all lawmaker, the Creator. This the Christ-Man acknowledged to Pilate: "Thou wouldst have no power at all over me were it not given thee from above" (Jn. 19:11). St. Paul emphasizes his Master's teaching: "Obey your superiors and be subject to them" (Hebr. 13:17), as does the first pope, St. Peter: "Servants, be subject to your masters in all fear, not only to the good and moderate, but also to the severe" (1 Pet. 2:18). And St. Paul gives the only reason for obedience: love of God, the authority in all authorities: "Let everyone be subject to the higher authorities; for there exists no authority except from God. . . . Therefore he who resists authority resists the ordinance of God" (Rom. 13:1-3). "Obey your masters according to the flesh [the government] . . . as you would Christ: not serving to the eye as pleasing men, but as slaves of Christ, doing the will of God from your heart, giving your service with good will as to the Lord and not to men" (Eph. 6:5-8).

St. Peter has the same and only valid reason for obedience, love

of God: "Be subject to every human creature for God's sake, whether
to the king as supreme, or to governors as sent through him" (1 Pet.
2:13). This was the teaching of the ancient Book of Wisdom (6:3–5):
"Give ear, you that rule the people . . . for power is given you by
the Lord, and strength by the most High . . . ministers of his
kingdom."

The New Testament is the "law of the Spirit," the law of God's
love for men, making them through grace the adopted children of
God and the brothers and sisters of Christ. It is probably rarely
realized by most readers of Scripture that when God's action on man
is expressed as effected through the Holy Spirit, generally it is God
as love operating on man. We should be alert to the significance of
"the Spirit" as love; and if we are, many of the inspired passages
will glow with enthralling meaning for our mind and heart.

The psalmist looked on law as given by love, the divine lawgiver:
"The Lord is sweet and righteous; therefore he will give a law to
sinners in the way" (Ps. 24:8). Hence the psalmist's deep love for
the law of God's love: "The law of thy mouth is good to me, above
thousands of gold and silver" (Ps. 118:72).

Ineffably more, the law of Christ is the law promulgated as love.
This law, which God foretold through Isaias, "shall go forth from
me" (51:4). It goes forth from God in the procession of the Holy
Spirit. It is the law that the Heart of God "writes in the heart of
man," love calling for love: "for the law was given through Moses;
grace and truth came through Jesus Christ" (Jn. 1:17).

The law of love is the Holy Spirit — or as St. Paul says: "The law
of the Spirit of Life in Christ Jesus has delivered me from the law
of sin and of death" (Rom. 8:2). Under law man must be. God
intends him to be under the law of love, the Holy Spirit. "To this
end was the gospel preached even in the dead that they may be
judged indeed as men in flesh, but may live as God lives, in spirit"
(1 Pet. 4:6), that is, in love. If man rebels against this law, he does
not become lawless, free of all law. He then enters into the hard,
inexorable law of sanction, visited on him by his very abused nature
and by love, the rejected Holy Spirit. St. Paul warns against such a
calamity: "He who rejects these things [laws of Christ] rejects not

man, but God, who has also given His Holy Spirit [love] to us" (1 Thess. 4:8).

Man is a sad being when he rejects love in his life, above all when he rejects the love that is the Holy Spirit. "Do not grieve the Holy Spirit of God, in whom you were sealed for the day of redemption" is the admonition of St. Paul (Ephes. 4:30). The same earnest warning is given by Christ that man cannot despise the love that is God the Holy Spirit, and that as long as he does so, he will never be forgiven: "I say to you that . . . blasphemy against the Spirit will not be forgiven" (Mt. 12:32). He explains this by the fact that the Spirit, God as love, in the soul is the good tree which alone will bear the good fruit intended from man. "Either make the tree good and its fruit good, or make the tree bad and its fruit bad" (ibid. 33).

11. A Father's Love

God has not forged the irons of a determinist universe on our powers of heart, mind, and body. He has bound us, indeed, but with the bonds of His love, bonds which we freely and honorably carry. "Love," says Bossuet, "is something that subdues our hearts and brings them under the rule of another, something that makes us depend on that other and rejoice in our dependence."[35]

"There is no [servile] fear in love; but perfect love casts out fear" (1 Jn. 4:18). Well did God compare His love for the human being with the love of a devoted father for his babe. "Whom the Lord loveth he chastiseth: and as a father in the son he pleaseth himself" (Prov. 3:12). He has really poured into our being from His own being a participation in the stream of His own life. In us He sees His own natural Son, the Word, being in being, life in life. He sees His Christ indwelling in our persons, divinely animating our actions and transfusing them with the dignity and worth of the actions of the divine adopted child of God.

Christ dwells frequently on His Father's love for Him, not only

---

[35] Serm. 2 de Assumptione, 2.

inasmuch as He is the identical God in the person of the Word, but also as He is the human Christ in the Word:

> The Father loves the Son, and has given all things into his hand (Jn. 3:35).
> For the Father loves the Son, and shows him all that he himself does (*ibid.*, 5:20).
> For this reason the Father loves me, because I lay down my life . . . (*ibid.* 10:17).

> The Son who is in the bosom of the Father (*ibid.* 1:18).

Incorporated, more intimately than we can know, in the Word through grace, we are incorporated in the Father's love of the Word in Christ, who also loves us with the same love, since He does whatever the Father does (cf. *ibid.* 5:19).

> As the Father has loved me, I also have loved you. Abide in my love (*ibid.* 15:9).
> Father, I will that where I am, they also, whom thou hast given me may be with me; in order that they may behold my glory, which thou hast given me, because thou hast loved me before the creation of the world. . . . And I have made known to them thy name, and will make it known, in order that the love with which thou hast loved me may be in them, and I in them (*ibid.* 17:24–26).

The inspired theme of the first part of St. Paul's Letter to the Ephesians (1:3–7) is this: In gratuitous love, the whole dispensation of God for the human race was eternally planned to take place by our becoming His co-children with and through Christ:

> Blessed be the God and Father of our Lord Jesus Christ, who has blessed us with every spiritual blessing on high in Christ. Even as he chose us in him before the foundation of the world, that we should be holy and without blemish in his sight in love. He predestined us to be adopted through Jesus Christ as his sons, according to the purpose of his will, unto the praise of the glory of his grace, with which he has favored us in his beloved Son.

"Can a woman forget her infant, so as not to have pity on the son of her womb?" With incomparably deeper meaning than in the Old Testament, in which God says this of the chosen people, He declares in these same words His parental love for His chosen people "in Christ," His "people of acquisition" of the New Testament;

"and if she should forget, yet will I not forget thee! Behold I have graven thee in my hands" (Isa. 49:15, 16). Our hands are always before our eyes; and "to engrave on His hands" was God's Hebrew expression for the fact that we are always before His eyes and are the object of His ever-constant fatherly love, much as the newborn babe is in the mind and concern of the mother. Such is God, says Blessed Angela de Foligno:

> Neither a mother enfolding her child in her arms nor anybody else can be imagined as embracing a beloved person with the ineffable love with which God embraces the human soul. He clasps it to Himself with a tenderness and affection that can be believed only by one who has experienced it.[36]

God is Father in three realms: first, in the realm of triune being by the Word's eternal Sonship in which we participate; second, in the realm of supernatural being by our participation in divine life through grace; third, in the realm of natural created being by our reception of likeness to our Creator. The Greek idiom of St. Paul makes it clear that we are so to understand His words: "I bend my knees to the Father of our Lord Jesus Christ, from whom all fatherhood in heaven and on earth receives its name" (Eph. 3:14-15); thus he declares God to be Father in all realms: "in heaven and on earth." The Greek words "all fatherhood" mean the source of all derivation of childhood.[37]

Isaias teaches the Jews the natural Fatherhood of God: "O Lord, thou art our father, and we are clay: and thou art our maker, and we all are the works of thy hands" (64:8); and often before the age of grace we find divinely inspired and touching expression of God's Fatherhood as Creator:

> The Lord thy God hath carried thee, as a man is wont to carry his little son (Deut. 1:31).
> That thou mayst consider in thy heart, that, as a man traineth up his son, so the Lord thy God hath trained thee up (ibid. 8:5).
> Is not he thy father, that hath possessed thee, and made thee, and created thee? (ibid. 32:6.)
> Be ye children of the Lord your God (ibid. 14:1).

---

[36] Livre, ed. P. Doncouer, S.J., p. 108.
[37] Cf. La théologie de St. Paul, F. Prat, S.J., 14 ed. (Paris: Beauchesne, 1929), Vol. 1, c. 2, p. 166.

At least from this time (of need) call to me: Thou art my father
(Jer. 3:4).

And I said: Thou shalt call me father and thou shalt not cease to
walk after me (*ibid.* 3:19).

For I am a father to Israel (Jer. 31:9).

Hear, O ye heavens, and give ear, O earth, for the Lord hath
spoken. I have brought up children, and exalted them: but they
have despised me (Isa. 1:2).

And creature man speaks to his Creator Father:

For thou art our father . . . thou, O Lord, art our father, our
redeemer; from everlasting is thy name (Isa. 63:16).

O Lord, father, and sovereign ruler of my life! (Ecclus. 23:1.)

Now that, in faith, we have eaten of the New Testament's tree
of knowledge, now that we have partaken of the eternal flow of life
from the Father to the Son, we have been brought familiarly nigh
to the inaccessible throne of God as His adopted children: "Creation
itself also will be delivered from its slavery to corruption into the
freedom of the glory of the sons of God" (Rom. 8:21).

Pronounced as they are, Christ's assertions of our participation in
the Sonship of the Word without the assurance of the infallible
guidance of the Church would be open to minimizing of their awe-
some grandeur. The unquestionable explanation of the teaching
Church, founded by Christ precisely because of such necessity,
assures us of correct understanding of Christ's revelation of God as
our Father in grace, with Christ as our divine, even more than our
human, brother. This brotherhood with the Word Christ should be
the constant inspiration and genial warmth of our lives.

In his Letters, St. John adds greater explicitness to his gospel of
man's divine sonship in the adoption of grace; and St. Paul unfolds
the "mystery from the foundation of the world" in still greater
detail and frequency. But ultimately we must come to the knees of
Mother Church, wise with participation in the wisdom of her
spouse, the indwelling Holy Spirit, and listen to her who wrote the
inspired New Testament as a part of her divinely protected teaching
and tradition. She tells us with explicit certainty that we, her chil-

dren, are the adopted divine children of the infinite Father, born and living by participation in His divine life.

From the time of Christ on, in the era of grace, "Father" is the proper name for God, not only because of His transcendent dignity as Creator of our humanity, but especially because of His second creation of our divinity through the grace of Christ. During the era of the dominance of original sin, God was usually spoken of, and to, as the Creator "Lord."

When Christ spoke of, and to, God — and in that He was giving us an example to be followed — He used the terms "My Father," "our Father," or simply, "the Father." Sometimes it is not clear whether He is speaking exclusively as the eternally begotten Son, or whether He also expressly includes us as the adopted fellow children of God. Again, when there is question of God as Father of man, sometimes it is not clear whether He speaks of God our Father, inasmuch as He is our Creator, or expressly as our Father through participation in His divine Life through grace. In many expressions, however, all of these meanings are individually clear.

III. LOVE'S LIKENING

1. Love Assimilative

There is nothing that likens two persons to one another as does love. Human love likens soul to soul; and the soul is the principal constituent of human nature. Through grace, the Creator's love has astoundingly likened human nature to divine nature. The more our will, or love, freely but with His help, likens our beings and actions to God's will and being, the more His grace assimilates and fuses us with God, while, of course, we retain our own identity. Our every action and every creature involved in our action are meant to be only means to our greater likeness to God, which makes possible our greater union with Him in love and grace.

St. Bernard urges on us this sole way of assimilation with and in God:

> The converted soul comes to the Word to be formed anew by Him and conformed to Him. By what means? By love. Such conformity marries the soul to the Word; that is, the soul, like to the Word by Grace, makes itself more like to Him by its will, loving Him as it is loved by Him.[1]

By its representation of the known object the mind, in a way, is made like to what is known. But this transformation of the mind is not transformation of the person or character, which takes place only in the will's love. St. Bonaventure, after St. Dionysius and Hugh of St. Victor, gives the reason: "Because love unites, it is said to transform the lover into the beloved object."[2]

Union can take place in so far as two things are alike. Love, union of wills, is the intensest of unions, since it is the profoundest

---

[1] *In Cant.* 83, 2, 3.
[2] *Sent.* 2, 15, 1, 1; passim.

of likenesses. Thus, in a sense, the lover becomes the beloved, by taking on himself the nature or "form" of the beloved in taking on the will of the beloved. Love the good, and you become good. Love the base, and you become base. An evil man may know holiness better than a good man; but he does not become good by his knowledge, while he does become good by his love of the good. Consequently, the degree of likeness to the beloved is reciprocally equivalent to the degree of union of love.

Knowledge, likeness of mind, does not lead us to act and will as the known object does; but love's likeness leads us to act and will as the beloved acts and wills. God's love of us does not change Him, but it makes us like to Him. So St. Bonaventure teaches:

> . . . divine love is not the love of affection inclining God to another being but rather inclining another to Himself. Hence, divine love transforms and conforms the beloved to the loving one, rather than vice-versa.[3]

The loved good in its attainment, says Aquinas, is a perfecting or "form," for the capacity of the lover.[4] Fulfillment of love by the good loved is a transformation of the good into the lover and of the lover into the good as his acquired perfection. Love is perfecting. "Love is unifying and concretionary," says Dionysius, and the loved good is formative of the lover, somewhat like the incorporation of "form" into "matter."[5]

As all love is likeness through union of wills, it is not strange that our Lord instructed St. Catherine of Siena that perfect love for Him, for which she yearned, is perfect likeness of her will with His:

> To love Me perfectly three things are necessary. In the first place, to purify and direct the will in its temporal loves and bodily attachments, so that nothing passing or perishable is loved except because of love of Me. . . . I have made and given them to you that you should learn a better idea therefrom of My limitless Goodness and so love Me yet more.
> In the second place, put My honor and My glory as the sole end of your thoughts, of your actions and of all that you do . . .

---

3 *Sent.* 3, 32, 1, 2.
4 Cf. *Summa,* 1–2, 26, 2.
5 *PG* 3, 713.

so that everyone that you meet may know, love and worship Me like you and with you. . . .

In the third place, if you do that which I am going to tell you now, you will have reached a consummate perfection and nothing will be wanting in you. It is the attainment of an ardently desired and perseveringly sought disposition of the soul, in which you are so closely united with Me and your will is so perfectly conformed to My perfect Will, that you never wish, not only evil, but even good which I do not wish. . . .[6]

We must keep in mind, while reading this advice of our Lord on her abandonment of all her care to Him, that Catherine was not concerned merely with herself. She was a woman of many important cares and activities, such as inducing the Pope to return to Rome from Avignon, counseling him in Rome, and supplying the needs of the poor.

There is much to give us pause in Plato's explanation of the reason for the defectiveness of creature knowledge. The subject knowing and loving and the object known and loved, once one in God, he says, became separated on going out from Him as creatures. Thus entered the defect into love and knowledge. St. Thomas christianizes this doctrine:

The soul is made like to God by Grace. Hence for a divine Person (the Son or the Holy Spirit) to be sent to anyone by Grace, there must needs be a likening of the soul to the divine Person Who is sent, by some gift of Grace. Because the Holy Spirit is love, the soul is assimilated to the Holy Spirit by the gift of charity. Hence the mission of the Holy Spirit is according to the gift of charity. The Son is the Word, not any sort of word, but the word breathing forth love. Hence, St. Augustine says: "The Word of which we speak is knowledge joined with love" (De Trin. 9, 10). Thus the Son is sent, not in accord with any and every kind of intellectual perfection, but in accord with intellectual union which breaks forth into the affection of love.[7]

Through grace we shall happily return from the original separation of sin into the perfect love and knowledge of heaven, where all our love and knowledge will be the participation of God who is the

---

[6] *Dialogue on Perfection.*
[7] *Summa*, 1, 43, 5, 2.

subject knowing and loving Himself, the very object which He knows and loves. It is the nature of divine love in creation to make the beloved creature like unto itself, with various degrees of natural likeness rising to the culmination of likeness in the divine assimilation of grace. God begets His substantial Image, the Word, who in grace makes us His echo. This is the "deification" of man, of which the Fathers speak so rapturously. It is not merely a supernatural similarity to God; it is a mystic divine union with Him, which is the constitution and inseparable cause of this divine similarity between creature and Creator. Born in love, in the Holy Spirit, to a divine life, man's infinitely distant lowliness is made nigh to the Most High; and it exists now divinely in God.

Love's divine assimilation of the lover into the beloved in grace is described by our Lord to the mystical St. Mary Magdalen de Pazzi:

> The iron, which comes forth from the furnace, shines, sparkles and burns like a fire . . . and the same thing happens to a soul in this furnace of love, wherein it is united to My Word, who is the fire which inflames and who came to cast fire upon earth in order to enkindle all hearts. Within this furnace, where the Holy Spirit makes the fire burn ever more ardently, the soul is so consumed by this fire that, instead of being merely human, it becomes wholly divine, transformed into Me and made one thing with Me through charity. . . . It then becomes more perfect in its works, more lofty in its concepts, more ardent in its love, so that we need only to glance at that soul to see that it belongs to Me and to recognize in it the Author of its transformation. Let a soul change itself otherwise, as it may, it will never recover the primitive perfection of its being [before Original Sin], except by being transformed into Me. Only then will it conform to the idea which I had when I created it.[8]

Since the Word tells us that His love for us is similar to the love of the Father for Him: "As the father has loved me, I also have loved you" (Jn. 15:9), and since the Father loves the Son because He is like the Father, we must conclude that we are like the Son, to be loved like the Son.

St. Irenaeus says: "Because of His love, He was made what we are, so that He might perfect us into what He is,"[9] namely, divine children

---

[8] *Oeuvres*, 4, c. 19.
[9] *Heresies*, 5, Pref.

living by participation in the Life of the Son of God. As infinite
Truth, God can love, Luther notwithstanding, only to the degree
that an object is lovable. If He loves us so ardently and devotedly, if
He embraces our persons in divine union with Himself, we must
conclude that we have a wonderful divine worth and beauty, a worth
and a beauty like unto His own.

"Love either finds the beloved like to itself or makes the beloved
like to itself," says St. Augustine. Certainly, we did not give ourselves our great beauty of nature; for we came from nothing, and
hence can give ourselves nothing by ourselves, even though it be our
natural endowments, inherited, acquired, or both. Much less can
we give ourselves the supernatural and divine beauty and endowments
of grace.

"Because Thou hast loved me, Thou hast made me lovable": this
precious gem of thought comes from St. Augustine, the lapidary of
Christian truth.[10] It is a sparkling jewel, in which the word *lovable*
has the two facets of "beloved of divine Love" and "participator in
divine love." In this brilliant apothegm Augustine has enclosed the
whole wealth of grace, asserting in it both our supernatural elevation
to participation in divine nature and love, and also the primacy
of grace in beginning, sustaining, and perfecting this supernatural
state and its activity.

The beauteous sun, rising on the life of the day, gives the beauty
which it sees. God, the light and life of the soul, gives the beauty
which He contemplates and loves in the soul, namely, the participation of Himself.

> "What happy comelinesses rise
> Beneath Thy beautifying eyes! . . .
> Yea, the gazes, blissful Lover,
> Make the beauties they discover."
> (F. Thompson, *Orient Ode*)

Then, the initially gratuitous assimilating Presence must be enhanced by our own efforts in grace, as St. Francis de Sales, the Doctor
of love, instructs us:

> In gazing at Him often by meditation, your whole soul becomes
> filled with Him; you will learn His characteristics, and you will

―――――
[10] *On St. John's Gospel,* tr. 102, 16, 28.

form your actions after the model of His actions. . . . The infant through force of hearing its mother and of stammering along with her, learns to speak her language; and we by remaining near our Lord in meditation and by hearing His words, seeing His actions and experiencing His affections, learn with His grace to speak, to act, and to wish as He does.[11]

It has often been remarked that marriage sometimes joins a man and woman who are unlike one another, but long and close association gradually likens them. They come to act alike, to talk alike, to think alike, and even, as far as possible, to look alike. This is the necromancy of likening love.

> Not like to like, but like in difference.
> Yet, in the long years, liker must they grow. . . .
> Till, at the last, she set herself to man
> Like perfect music unto perfect words. . . .
> Distinct in individualities,
> But like each other, e'en as those who love.
>   (Tennyson, *The Princess*)

We are drawn to the infinite Goodness because of our great difference in our absolute need of Him — we all-dependent, He all self-sufficient; He the boundless welling source of love, beauty, power, wealth, and honor; we all recipient. By our increasing union with Christ in grace, we are increasingly like Him. More and more, we think as He does, we will as He does, we talk, we act as He does; but still more wonderfully, we are like Him more and more in His divine nature in which we more and more participate, divinely thinking and willing and acting, even as divine children become like their divine Father: "although the print be small, the matter and the copy of the Father."[12]

2. *"One Becomes That on Which He Feeds His Heart"* (Upanishads)

Not only does divine Love liken us to God in grace by sharing the divine nature with us, but it also has likened God Incarnate to us

---

[11] *Devout Life*, 2, 1.
[12] Shakespeare, *Winter's Tale*, 2, 3, 92.

in sharing our human nature and in making our divine likeness with Him possible. In Christ, divine and human nature say to one another with the assurance of love: "All I have is thine."

God's purpose for man is a union of love with Him far surpassing even that of spouse with spouse. Man, St. Paul tells us, shall be so united in love with his spouse that "he shall leave his father and mother and shall cleave to his wife; and the two shall become one flesh" (Eph. 5:31). This marital union the Apostle uses as a pale image of "the great sacrament," or mystery, of the union of God with man in grace. "He who cleaves to the Lord," he affirms, "is one spirit with him" (1 Cor. 6:17).

Love makes us as melted wax which takes the form of the object it touches. As St. Augustine observes, "Each one is what his love is. If you love earth, you are earth. If you love God — what am I to say? — you are God [divine]. What greater excellence can you ascribe to the love of God than the power to transform men into God?"[13] So the prophet Osee (9:10) declares that the wicked become abominable, like the things they love. Human love makes the lover like the beloved by sharing only in the sentiments of the beloved, such as joy, sadness, suffering, loss, or gain. Thus the lover ceases to live his own life and mentally and sympathetically lives the life of the beloved. Hence Plato notes that he who truly loves seems to have died to himself and to live in the beloved. Love of God, not only by a moral union, shares in the sentiments of God, but also by a physical union, shares in His very being and nature; and thus we live divine life, while He lives in our human life: "Christ liveth in me."

As a true spouse leading human nature into the home of His divinity, God unbelievably wishes to have His goods in common with His creature by absorbing it into His nature, while preserving its own entity. He makes the human supernaturally patient of the divine. He wishes, with divine fullness, to possess our human beings and divinely to be possessed by our beings.

Divine Love's assimilation of the beloved begets a similarity which Christ explains through the simile of the vine. The branch is similar to the vine because when grafted on the vine it lives, not of its own life, but of the life of the vine flowing through it. Life is the

---

[13] *In 1 Joan.* 2, 14; PL 35, 1997.

principle and source of unity. So in grace we are received into God and form a union with Him, living with participation in His Life which vivifies our being. The grafted branch is wholly assimilated by the life of the vine and exists no longer by itself and for itself but in the vine and for the vine. Man in grace lives in God and for God, love making the finite like the Infinite.

On the hills around the Jesuit novitiate at Los Gatos, California, where I became a Jesuit, all the grape vines had to be uprooted, as they had become infected with phyloxera. French vine scions were grafted into American wild vine roots which were immune to the disease; and new vineyards were planted for the making of sacramental wine. The French scion changed the life of the wild root into its own life and produced French grapes. Similarly, if we ingraft the love of God into our human loves, it will change our human life into divine life and it will bear divine fruits in us.

St. Francis de Sales teaches that love is the absorption and elevation of our will in the will of God:

> What becomes of the light of the stars when the sun appears on the horizon. Certainly it does not perish; but it is ravished and absorbed into the sun's sovereign light with which it is happily mingled and allied. And what becomes of man's will when it is entirely delivered up to God's pleasure? It does not entirely perish; but it is lost and dispersed in the Will of God that it does not appear and has no other will than the Will of God.[14]

The sun does not "scatter into flight the stars before him from the field of night." Starlight comes to us in the day, but permeated and empowered by the radiance of the sun. Our human beings, our lives, our actions, in grace's supernatural state and activity, remain in all their human reality, but permeated and empowered by the divinity in which we participate.

Our divine Lover fills us through grace with participation in the divine being which is begotten eternally by the Father and dwells corporally through hypostatic union as one person in Christ: "In him dwells all the fullness of the Godhead bodily, and in him . . . you have received of that fullness" (Col. 2:9–10). St. John Chrysostom explains this passage: "You have nothing other than Christ; as the

---

[14] *Treatise on the Love of God.*

divinity dwells [by nature] in Him, so it dwells [by grace] in you"[15];
and Theophilus similarly: "When our nature was joined by the
divine nature [in Christ], we also become participants in the same
divine nature."[16]

It is the glorious divinity as the only-begotten of the Father which
is full of grace and truth; and of His fullness we have all received,
grace for grace (Jn. 1:14, 16). On this passage St. John Chrysostom
notes that the divinity of Christ is this "fullness," by observing that
Moses gave the law as a servant of God, but that grace "was made"
or "took place" through Christ as the Master of Grace. It is the
divine person of Christ in both His divine nature and His human
nature which makes Him the Head of the Church, which "indeed is
his body, the [messianic] completion of him who fills all [his members]
with all" (Eph. 1:23) — with divine life and divine powers to glorify
God. Our ideal of loving assimilation to Christ, says St. Paul, is to
attain the intended fullness of the divine life of Christ in us. Thus
we develop Christ in us "until we attain to the unity of the faith
and of the deep knowledge of the Son of God, to perfect manhood,
to the mature measure of the fullness of Christ" (*ibid.* 4:13).

3.   Love Transforming

> Learn that the flame of everlasting love
> Doth burn ere it transform. . . .
> (Newman, *The Dream of Gerontius.*)

"Unless the grain of wheat falls into the ground and dies, it remains
alone. But if it dies, it brings forth much fruit" (Jn. 12:24–25). The
grain of wheat must lose itself in the ground. The human soul must
lose itself in God in order to be transformed into the new divine life
of grace which He gives. The soul must lose above all its rebellious
will in the sovereign will of God. If the grain of wheat remain only
a grain of wheat, it will lose its life. It cannot live an independent

---

[15] Quoted by Knabenbauer, *In Col.*, Lethielleux, Paris, 1912, p. 328.
[16] *Ibid.*

LOVE'S LIKENING   169

life of its own. We may not live only human lives; we must spring
up into divine Life. Thus only can we be changed like the wheat
grain into a life of new activity, new beauty, and new fruitfulness.
The life of love springs from the death of opposing self.

The distinctive sign of Christ our Redeemer is the cross; and to
be "in Christ" we must take up the cross of denial of tendencies that
impudently go athwart His will. This is the ABC of the doctrine of
St. John of the Cross, Doctor of the spiritual life:

> Before this divine fire of love enters into the soul and is united
> with it in its substance through completed and perfect purgation
> and purity, this flame which is the Holy Spirit is in the soul,
> wounding it and destroying and consuming the imperfections of
> its bad habits. This is the operation of the Holy Spirit by which It
> disposes the soul for divine union and substantial transformation in
> God through love.[17]
>
> These souls, God told St. Catherine of Siena, thrown into the
> furnace of My love, no part of their will remaining outside but the
> whole of them being inflamed by Me, are like a brand wholly con-
> sumed in the furnace, so that no one can take hold of it to
> extinguish it, because it has become fire. In the same way, no one
> can seize those souls nor draw them outside of Me because they
> are made one thing with Me through grace; and I never withdraw
> Myself in sentiment . . . as in the case of those whom I am leading
> on to perfection.[18]

St. John of the Cross smelts his spirituality in the reducing furnace
of a love of God that is fiercely purifying before it can be intimately
alloying. He understands the union of "the state of marriage of the
soul with God" as a consciousness of grace's participation in God
and in His omnivalent love; but it is only consequent on the suppression of any will in us contrary to the will of God. This suppression takes place in what this Mystical Doctor of the Church calls
"the passive night of the soul," which he illustrates by a figure which
may have lost some of its vividness for us children of an oil-and-gas-
burning century, who may have seen little or no green wood burning:

> It is fitting to note here that this purgative and loving knowledge,
> or divine light, of which we speak in this canto, is in the soul

---

17 *The Living Flame of Love,* 1, 4, 19.
18 *Dialogue,* 78.

purifying and disposing it in order to unite it with Himself perfectly, in the same way as fire is in the wood, in order to transform
the wood into itself. Material fire, applying itself to the wood, first
of all begins to dry the wood, forcing out the moisture and making it
weep forth the water which it contains in itself. Then it gradually
darkens the wood, black and ugly, and even malodorous. Con-
tinuing its drying, it proceeds, little by little, to take out and
eject all the ugly and dark appearances, which the wood holds
in opposition to the fire. Finally, beginning to set the wood on
fire outside and heating it, the fire comes to transform the wood
into itself and to render it as beautiful as the fire itself. . . .

In this same way, we are to philosophize on the divine Fire
of Love in contemplation, which, before it transforms the soul
into itself, first purifies it from all opposing characteristics.[19]

It can well be that John was influenced, as was his close friend,
Teresa of Avila, by the spirituality of his countryman Loyola, as
John was born in the year 1542 while Ignatius died in 1556, at
which time his spirituality was well known in Spain. The spirit
of transformation of will into the divine will, under the figure of
the green wood transformed into fire, is the spirit and apogee of
the Spiritual Exercises of Ignatius: expressed in the "Suscipe":

Accept and take, dear Lord, my liberty!
Take all! my will, my mind, my imagery!
All I possess to Thee I here consign:
All gavest Thou; all I restore; 'tis Thine.
All that I am and do, 'neath Thy love's sway
Do Thou dispose and rule in Thy will's way.
Wealth that suffices, glory in high place,
Give me in giving but Thy love and Grace.

The poet of divine love, no less than the poet of human love, sees
the ideal life as that in which two feel: We are two with only one
heart. In fact, from basement to pinnacle, St. John of the Cross
designs spiritual perfection about a framework of higher and higher
likeness of the human will to the divine will.

When the soul comes to have likeness to God . . . this is supernatural union . . . the will of the soul and the Will of God are
one in conformity, one holding nothing repugnant to the other . . .
the soul remains transformed in God through love. . . .

19 *Loc. cit.*, 2, 10.

To love is to work to despoil oneself for God's sake of all that is not God. Then the soul remains illuminated [like a window-pane] and transformed in God; and God communicates to it His supernatural being in such a way that the soul seems to be God Himself and it has what He Himself has. This union is effected when God gives the soul the supernatural mercy that all the things of God and of the soul are the same in participating likeness. The soul then appears more like God than like a soul — it is even God by participation. However it remains its own being naturally as distinct from God's Being as before the union, although it is transformed, as the windowpane remains distinct from the light while illuminated by the light.[20]

As pagan Plato urged in a cadre of thought very different from ours, we must attain "the likeness of God" in so far as reason can guide us to the virtues:

We should flee from here [the deluding attractiveness of earth] to there [the truth of God] as quickly as possible; and this flight is our likening to God as far as is possible; and to become like Him is to become holy and just with wisdom.[21]

Augustine of Hippo, once a follower of Plato, finds as a Christian the real means of ascent to God in the Godman, the divine Logos, the Savior of mankind. He explains how we ascend to God through Christ:

Let the same Paul tell us who is that Christ Jesus our Lord: ". . . we preach Christ, the Power of God and the Wisdom of God." Does not Christ Himself say: "I am the Truth?" . . . To Him we adhere through sanctification [likeness in Grace]. Sancti-fied, we are inflamed with full and integral love of God, by which alone it is effected that we do not turn from God and that we are made rather like to Him than like to this world. "For he pre-destined us," says the same Apostle, "to be conformed to the image of His Son."[22]

Transformation into "conformity with the Son" of God requires that while we remain our human selves we are metamorphosed into divine human beings. The larva is metamorphosed into the bee. While it retains its own continuous being in the transformation, its

---

[20] *Active Night of the Soul*, 12, 5.
[21] *Theaetetus*, 176A.
[22] *Morality of the Church*, 13, 22; *PL* 32, 1321.

manifestations as a bee are different from those of a larva. While
man retains his human being in his transfiguration of grace, his
human manifestations become also divine and participate in God's
self-manifestations. This is a metaphor used by St. Francis de Sales:

> Silkworms change their beings and from worms become butterflies.
> Bees are born worms, then become nymphs crawling on their feet;
> and at last they become flying bees. We do the same, Theotimus,
> if we are spiritual; for we foresake our natural life to live a more
> eminent life above ourselves, hiding all this new life in God with
> Christ, who alone sees, knows and bestows it. Our new life is
> heavenly love which quickens and animates our soul; and this love
> is wholly hidden in God and in divine things with God.[23]

Blessed Henry Suso, O.P. (1295–1366), makes it clear that love's
spiritual transformation of our person is, on our part, transformation
of our will into the will of the divine beloved:

> Lord tell me what remains to a blessed soul which has wholly
> renounced itself. Truth says: When the good and faithful servant
> enters into the joy of his Lord, he is inebriated by the riches of
> the house of God; for he feels, in an ineffable degree, that which
> is felt by an inebriated man. He forgets himself, he is no longer
> conscious of his selfhood; he disappears and loses himself in God,
> drowned in a great quantity of wine. For even as a drop of water
> disappears, taking the color and the taste of wine, so it is with
> those who are in full possession of blessedness. . . . Herein thou
> shalt find an answer to thy question. For the true renunciation
> and veritable abandonment of a man to the divine Will in this
> temporal world is an imitation and reduction of that self-
> abandonment of the Blessed, of which Scripture speaks: and this
> imitation approaches its model more or less, according as men
> are more or less united with God.
>   Remark well that which is said of the blessed: that they are
> . . . changed into another form, another glory, another power.
> What, then, is this other form, if it be not the divine Nature and
> the divine Being whereinto they pour themselves, and Which
> pours Itself into them, and becomes one thing with them? And
> what is that other glory, if it be not to be illuminated and made
> shining in the inaccessible Light? What is that other power, if
> it be not that, by means of his union with the divine Personality,
> there is given to man a divine strength and a divine power

---

[23] *Treatise on the Love of God,* 11, 9.

that he may accomplish all which pertains to his blessedness, and omit all which is contrary thereto? And thus it is, as has been said, that a man comes forth from his selfhood.[24]

4. Purifying Love

It has often been noted that two persons are friendly and well-known to each other for years; but as soon as their lives are unified in love, the two existences, hitherto lived apart, are now diffused into and colored by each other. Before we possess the unifying love of sanctifying grace, we love the Son of God as our infinitely remote Creator, "who dwells in light invisible," "whom no one can see and live." After we are caught up into the divine life, our pettiness is transfused with participation in the fullness of the divinity and we live divinely, glorifying God in our human actions, possessing God with the depth and ardor of divine love in human hearts.

When God gives the soul the grace of ardent love, it thinks that it has reached the definitive fullness of spiritual life, that nothing remains but to enjoy loving Him and being loved by Him, "in that new world which is the old" (Tennyson). Soon God's transforming love, wishing to make His beloved holy, immaculate, without spot or wrinkle, begins to teach the naïve soul what it is and how it is to make itself more lovable and acceptable in His eyes. Love then becomes purgative, consuming and perfecting. The soul must henceforth be, not only His, but also wholly His.

Then shackling bonds to one's own will and to creatures which tend to impede union with God are ruthlessly cut away. Then the long regulation of eccentric self is studied and carried out by focusing it more and more completely and exactly on its true center, the divine love and will. The only possible rival of God is self; and the soul wholly in love with God will be glad to show the primacy of God in its being and life by subjecting wayward self-will to Him with the most searching detail and completeness.

---

24 *Little Book of Eternal Wisdom*, transl. C. H. McKenna, O.P., Benziger, N. Y., 1889.

In its first ardor of love of God, the soul feels the joy of divine affection and passes over many things in itself which are either objectionable or incongruous with full union of love. Then begins the assimilation so noticeable in human love, whether of friendship or of spouses. In grace, God first makes us like Himself according to our degree of union of will and love. Then He seeks a high degree of His divinity in us by developing a consciousness of our many ways of seeking self regardless of Him, and by a more perfect canalization of all our activities and objectives through Him. To the loving soul, this redirection of its life, through the indwelling Christ, totally to the pleasure of God, becomes its absorbing interest. It soon reshapes other loves in which He is not loved as wholly out of place in its intimate relation with Him. This is the strong life of love, a life of giving and of sacrificing independent self. It gives up, despite the strongest contrary emotion, anything and everything which may be a barrier to complete mutual possession between God and itself.

> Love takes up the harp of life
>   And smites on all the chords with might,
> Smites the chord of Self that trembling
>   Passes tuneful out of sight.
>   (Tennyson, *Locksley Hall,* reworded.)

5. *"Then Go Forward"*

Love of God quickly begins to operate that magical effect of love which makes two lovers will the same. Before love, the soul sees with the focus of self-centeredness and from its own point of view; in love, it sees everything through the will of God the Beloved and from His point of view. In the eyes of the Father, through love we become more and more like His Son, who does "nothing else but His Father's will"; and the Son takes us more and more intimately unto Himself: "If anyone love me he will keep my word, and my Father will love him, and we will come into him and make our abode with him" (Jn. 14:23).

Love of man transformed God, so to speak, into a human being, so that love of Him would transform humans into divine beings. The psychology of love's transformation of the lover is happily expressed by St. John of the Cross:

> Love never arrives at perfection until the loving ones are so reduced to one that they are transfigured one into the other. Then love is wholly sound . . . desiring to be transfigured with the figure of Him of Whom it is only an outline, its Spouse, the Word, the Son of God, Who is, as St. Paul says (Hebr. 1, 3), "the effulgence of God's glory and the figure of His Substance." This Figure is what the soul ambitions in desiring to be transfigured in love.
>
> > See what is the dolor
> > Of love, that it is not contented
> > Except with the Presence and the Figure.
> > (Text of the Canticle, st. 16)[25]

It is an immense favor and grace to love God generously and to realize that, because of our mergence in God's nature, we are magnificently loved, with an infinite love that contains all nobility, tenderness, and ardor. All the spiritual life takes on a different aspect. The soul, under the eyes of the infinitely loving God, changes its apparently unchangeable slovenliness and weak sloth with surprising facility; its one thought is to make itself more lovable to its God. Like the snake sloughing off its skin in the warm sun, we slough off with ease, in the warm sunlight of His presence, those inveterate habits of defects and sins which have grown to be so intimate a part of our being. The labors that are loved, observes St. Augustine, are by no means burdensome, but even are pleasant, such as the labors of hunting, trapping, fishing, harvesting, trafficking, or playing some game. There is interest in what is loved. Where one loves, one does not labor; and if one labors, one does not love.[26]

Everyone, whatever be his cares and possessions, should express his love of God in the generous manner told by St. John of the Cross:

> My soul has employed itself and all its possessions in this service. Now I guard no flock, nor have I other office; for now my exercise is in loving alone.[27]

[25] *Spiritual Canticle,* tr. A. Peers Vol. 2, p. 172. [27] *Spiritual Canticle.*
[26] Cf. *De civit. Dei,* 21, 26.

In other words, all a person's interests, no matter how many and varied, are attended to, as an expression of love of God. This is love's rigorous detachment — not that we do nothing but commune with the beloved God, but that, busy as we may be, all our purposes and occupations are to express our centric love for Him. As in magnanimous St. Joan of Arc, our sentiment of love of God is that "I would fain be to the eternal Goodness what his own hand is to a man."

Often a very small obstacle hinders great sanctity. Bl. Francis Perez de Godoi, born at Torrijos, in the diocese of Toledo, felt strongly, during the "Exercises," the call of God to leave court life and to enter the Society of Jesus. At the beginning he found this call extremely hard to obey, and one of the difficulties seemed to him fairly insurmountable. He found in his soul sufficient magnanimity to give up for the love of God his noble station, his wealth and comfort. But how could he bring himself to sacrifice his superb mustaches, in which he took great pride as a sign of masculine valor? At length divine inspiration proved stronger. The young man, armed with a pair of scissors, ruthlessly cut off his hirsute adornment; and persuaded, that, after such a sign of parting with his courtly world, it was impossible to return to his family, he insisted on immediate entrance into the Society of Jesus.

A "magnificent gesture" of love is all well and good, only if it is an incident in an everyday life of love. Such was the gesture of love for Christ of His simple spouse, St. Rose of Lima, only an incident in a complete life of love of Him. When the fleet of the Dutch heretics appeared off the coast of Peru in August, 1651, in the midst of the general consternation of Lima, St. Rose hastened to the altar steps of the church, there to defend her helpless Spouse and to give her life for Him. When the fleet departed amidst the general joy, she was sad that she could not pour out her life's blood for love of Christ at His feet where she daily prayed.

Some may be inclined to ask themselves: Was I created with my own temperament and judgment, with my personal preferences and will, with my own originality, only to crush it out — for instance, in common obedience to others in authority — only to throw back to God His special gifts to me? But let us reconsider this complaint in the light of the friendship of the soul with Christ, which Catholic authority supposes. Was not my free will given to me that I might make the most precious possible gift to my divine Friend, so that I have no will but His? Union and sacrifice of will is the essence of friendship. Was not my intellect given to me in order that all my knowledge might serve only to know my infinite Friend, in order that all my thinking might be in His way of thinking, in order that I might be totally under His will-control and His thought-control? Was not my power to love and to hate given to me to like only what He likes, to dislike only what is disliked by Him? The most dedicated love is the fiercest hate of opposition to the beloved. Only those know how to hate, and in the same degree, as they know how to love. Love is always war to the death on the enemies of the beloved.

Otherwise, do we not in effect say to God: I will give You some of myself and some of my life, but this or that I will not give You? Are we not the swimmer who wants to keep one foot on the bottom, who will not commit himself to the deep of total love with no other support? Are we not like the nun, Dame Morel, who, as we read in the history of the reform of the convent of Port Royal, was ready to give up all her luxuries inconsistent with her religious life, except one: the key to her little personal garden?

Yes, it is true, Catholicism does tend to disregard personal individualities, but only inasmuch as they are harmful and wrong, only to make them uniform with the perfect personality of Christ. This gift of ourselves to Christ is really Christ's gift of Himself to us; for He transforms and glorifies our nature and raises it to participation on His divine level. We then do not so much live our lives, as Christ lives them in us (Gal. 2:20). "We all . . . reflecting as in a mirror the glory of the Lord, are being transformed into his very image, from glory to glory, as through the Spirit of the Lord" (2 Cor. 3:18). Christ is the bee that processes all the diverse nectar of human beings into the one honey of participation in His same divine being, which is all diverse infinite perfections in one simplicity.

The love of God in Teresa of Avila constantly urged her and her religious daughters to generous expansion of soul for continually increasing union with God. The first reading proposed to the novice in Rodriguez' quaint and influential "Exercise of Christian Perfection" is the principle that, in love of God, not to go forward is to go backward. Real love's motto is *Ad altiora!* and this has been the prompting of the Mystical Body ever since Christ, its Head, proposed the counsel "if thou wouldst be perfect." *Le mieux est l'ennemi du bien* [The better is the enemy of the good]. Chivalrous Teresa thus stimulates her religious and us:

> Unless you strive after the virtues and practice them, you will never grow to be more than dwarfs. God grant that nothing worse than this happens; for, as you know, anyone who fails to go forward begins to go back; and love, I believe, can never be content to stay long where it is.[28]

St. Augustine similarly instructs his Christians:

> It must not be thought that those words of Christ: "Be perfect as your heavenly Father is perfect," were directed to virgins alone and not to the married, to widows but not to wives, to religious but not to those with families, to clerics but not to the laity. The entire Church must follow Jesus Christ and all the members of the Church, after the example of the Master, must carry the Cross and practice His teachings.[29]

Turinaz emphasizes the universality of the obligation to strive after perfection in love of God:

> The obligation to seek perfection binds all Christians; and the divine precepts which impose this obligation admit of no exceptions. They are universal, absolute and without restriction or reservation. Even the Old Law, which was but a preparation for the Gospel, states: "Thou shalt be perfect and without spot before thy Lord God" (Deut. 18:13), and "walk before Me and be perfect." St. Paul tells us: "Brethren, rejoice, be perfected" (2 Cor. 13:11); "even as He chose us before the foundation of the world, that we should be holy and without blemish in love" (Eph. 1:4). Are not the friends and children of God obliged to manifest the excellence of their dignity, through good works? Does not the divine Life itself, which has been communicated to us, and which unites

---

[28] *Interior Castle*, 7, 4.
[29] *Serm.* 47 de Divers. c. 7.

us intimately with the God of all sanctity, impose on us the obligation of striving for perfection?[30]

Love of God is a Commander whose standing command is that of General Patton to his troops before attack: "Go forward as far as you can; and then — go forward!" St. Francis de Sales, a celebrated strategist in the campaign of the spirit, says similarly:

> You learn to speak by speaking, to study by studying, to run by running, to work by working. And just so, you learn to love God by loving. All those who think to learn in any other way deceive themselves. If you wish to love God go on loving Him more and more. Never look back, press forward continually. Begin as a mere apprentice; and the very power to love will lead you on to become a master in the art. Thus those who have made most progress will continually press on, never believing that they have reached their end. For charity should go on increasing until we draw our last breath.[31]

6. I Rest, a Flute Laid on Thy Lips

Love is essentially union of persons. This union is personal only in the union of souls, and the union of souls reaches its peak in the peak of the soul: in union of wills, which is love. One may love another in varying degrees, and the degrees of love are the extent of the abandonment of self to the beloved. In love of God, the extent of identification of self with God's self, on our part, is indicated by the consequent extent of surrender of our personal desires to the good pleasure of the beloved.

When the "lover gives all for the beloved," he does so for the possession of the beloved in union of wills. Emotion may or may not be involved. It is a matter of the will at one with the will of the beloved. Understand it so, and there is no vagueness, but a precise definiteness, in the meaning of Scripture: "If a man should give all the substance of his house for love, he shall despise it as nothing"

---

30 *Vida Divina*, c. 5.
31 C. F. Camus, *The Spirit of St. Francis de Sales*, 1, 1, 2.

(Cant. 8:7). Neither attraction of creature, nor any suffering or misfortune can draw away the "naughted soul" from union with God's will in love. "Many waters cannot quench charity, neither can the floods drown it" (*ibid.*). After our Lord, St. Paul spells out how love of God is union of will with His will, by telling us in detail the virtues to be practiced and the vices to be avoided in love of God (1 Cor. 13). St. John is also down to earth, as well as in the seventh heaven, in his understanding of love of God: "He who keeps His word (will), in him the love of God is truly perfected" (1 Jn. 2:5).

Jalálu 'd Din (1207–1273), an eastern mystic, finely expresses love as the total cession of one's self and will to the beloved:

> With Thy sweet Will this will of mine
> Is one, as water mixed with wine. . . .
> I rest a flute laid on Thy lips,
> A lute I on Thy breast recline.[32]

According to Augustine, "human beings are nothing else than so many wills, or loves." Affectionate spirituality is the orthodox spirituality of all great souls. Affectionate emotion is the natural result of knowledge and appreciation of God. Man is a creature of emotion, as well as of thought. The sentiments of the heart enamored of God are the flowers of spirituality; but they must grow on the tree of firm faith and union with God's will; otherwise they are only paper flowers and cannot bear the fruit of self-sacrifice.

Writing, a mere series of signs expressing thought, has no value except inasmuch as it expresses thought. The greater value of the thought, and not the caligraphy, makes the greater value of the writing. Action, the expression of our will, gets all its moral value and worth, in the eyes of God and in truth, not from the grandeur of the action, but from our will in the action. Outside of the will, or love, actions are meaningless, empty, and worthless; and our will, or love, has all its value from its union with God's will. More than human marriage, the marriage of the soul with God is an "egoism of two" become one, "la vie à deux."

The unknown early English author of "The Epistle of Prayer" explains the soul's union with God in this same way:

---

[32] *The Festival of Spring*, tr. Hastie, p. 10.

I would that thou knew what manner of working it is that knitteth man's soul to God, and that maketh it one with Him in love and in accordance of will, after the word of St. Paul saying thus: *Qui adhaeret Deo, unus spiritus est cum Illo* . . . that is, though all that God and he be two and sere in kind, nevertheless, in Grace they are so knit together that they are one in spirit; for all this is one for one head of love and accordance of will . . . understanding that God shall be knitted with the ghostly glue of Grace on His party, and the lovely consent in gladness of spirit on thy party.[33]

"Before doing, learn to love." Activity is bulk, love is value in our lives. Not how long we live, not how great the activity of our lives, but how great the love in our lives determines their worth for eternity. A brief life of high love, like that of St. Stanislaus Kostka, may be a small package of rare diamonds. A long life of mediocre love may be a great quantity of coal, of value, indeed, but incomparable with diamonds, which are concentrated, crystalline coal. Among the eternal greats are the lives of many years of ordinary activities, "unnoticed and unsung" but magnificent in their love of God. Such a one was the Brother doorkeeper, St. Alphonsus Rodriguez, of whom Hopkins tells:

> Yet God . . .
> Could crowd career with conquest while there went
> Those years and years by of world without event
> That in Majorca Alphonsus watched the door.

The washerwoman's son, Fray Luis de Granada, dwells on this *multum in parvo,* much love and worth in a small life:

> This doctrine is very consoling for the poor ones, who have nothing to give, and for those who have neither education nor talent, and for the aged and sick who have little bodily strength. They can perform great deeds for God; for, without those other powers, they can love God much. He does much, who loves much. He gives much, who gives much of himself in love. He does much, who desires to do much; for, with God who sees the heart, the good will is not of less value than the good work.
> If you cannot do much, desire much and love much; and in that love you do much. If you are poor in riches to give alms,

---

[33] Cf. G. Gardner, *The Cell of Self-Knowledge,* Seven old English mystical works (London: Medieval Library, 1910), p. 88.

you are rich in love to desire to give them; and hold as certain that thus you have already given them.[34]

We are truly great if our interior life with God is great, small as our life in the exterior world may be. A bubble existence of magnificent appearance, without love of God within, eventually collapses unsupported. Created to lead both an external material life with others and an internal spiritual life with God, we are only half a human being — and by far the inferior half — if we do not live our interior life of union with God. We are like some gold coinage of the past. The exterior appearance of the gold coin was of little import; its weight of interior gold determined its value. Our love of God and union with Him is the gold in the shape of our lives.

If we do not live in the loving company of God, though we have multiple human company, we are fundamentally solitary and alone. Like St. Bernard we are, as he says, never less alone than when alone with God as the companion of our solitude.

> How sweet! how passing sweet is solitude!
> But grant me still a friend in my retreat,
> To whom I may whisper: sweet is solitude!
> (Cowper, *Retirement.*)

When our vision is not wholly or principally of the outward material world, the inner spiritual world "flashes on the inward eye, which is the bliss of solitude."

> Yea, in that ultimate heart's occult abode,
> To lie as in an oubliette of God,
> Or in a bower untrod
> Built by a secret lover for His spouse
> Sole choice is this your life allows.
> (Francis Thompson, *A Fallen Yew.*)

Of no one is it more absolutely and tragically true that "he is alone who does not love" than of him who does not love God.

---

[34] *Del Fin del Hombre*, 2, 22.

7. Unitive Love

Love's law that we give ourselves wholly to the beloved arises from
the infinite depths of the nature of God Himself, who perfectly and
in absolute fullness and unity of being is each of the three persons
of the Holy Trinity. Our love of God, in its self-giving, must be a
mirror of the threefold unity. In grace our love must be a participated enactment of the one act of loving of the Holy Trinity, in
and through the loving Christ.

The mystery of the union of the Holy Trinity is in the fact that
each person's attitude toward the others is: "My being is thy
being." All love strains, by the mere fact that it is created, to imitate
the creator love of the three who are one being, by seeking a oneness
with the beloved which says: "I am thyself."

Love's law of oneness of the two loving, in Arabian spirituality,
was expressed in the oft-quoted parable:

> The lover knocks at the door of the beloved; and a voice asks
> from within: "Who art thou?" "I am Ansar," he said; and the
> voice replied: "There is not room for me and thee in this house";
> and the door remained shut. Then the lover returned to the desert
> and fasted and prayed in solitude. After a year, he came back and
> knocked again at the door. Again, the voice asked: "Who art
> thou?" "I am thy brother," he answered; and the voice replied:
> "There is not room for me and thee in this house." After another
> year of fasting and prayer in the desert, the lover returned and
> once more knocked at the door. Once more the voice asked: "Who
> art thou?" He replied: "I am thyself"; and the door opened
> to him.

In grace, we say to God: "I am the participation of Thyself, whom
Thou lovest in my loving Thee." For so He wishes to be loved and
lover in all our loves of friends, in all our loves of spouse and
children, in all our loves of nature and of art, in all our loves of
social sympathy, in all our loves of wealth, honor, and pleasure. This
lover wishes to engross, absorb, and monopolize, in His Mystical
Body, all human being and life, so that He can say: "I am in thy-

self; and thou art in Me." "God is love, and he who abides in love abides in God, and God in him" (1 Jn. 4:16).

"All I have is thine," God challenges us. "I spared not even my own son, but delivered him up for you." Hence, concludes St. Paul, "How can he fail to grant us also all things with him?" (Rom. 8:32.) It is divine love's voice that challenges reciprocal giving:

> Hearken, O daughter, and see, and incline thy ear: and forget thy people and thy father's house. And the king shall greatly desire thy beauty; for He is the Lord thy God (Ps. 44:11–12).

Our giving of self to our beloved God, meeting God's boundless giving of Himself to us, is the climax of the mysticism of St. John of the Cross:

> The soul sees that God is truly hers, and that she possesses Him with hereditary possession, with ownership by right as adopted child of God by Grace, which God gave to her by giving Himself to her; and she sees that she can give and communicate Him, as her own possession. . . . So, she gives Him to her Beloved, Who is God Himself, Who gave Himself to her. In this, she pays God all she owes Him, inasmuch as she freely gives Him as much as she receives from Him.
>
> Because in this gift, which the soul makes to God, she gives Him the Holy Spirit, as her own possession with voluntary delivery, in order that He, and in herself, may love Himself as He deserves, the consequence is that the soul has inestimable delight and fruition; for she sees that she gives God, as her own possession, what is fit for God, according to His infinite Being. . . . And God is paid with that gift of the soul, Who would not be paid by less; and He receives it with gratitude, since the soul gives Him what is her own. And in that same gift, He loves the soul anew, while in that redelivery of God to the soul, the soul also loves God anew.
>
> Thus, between God and the soul, there is actually formed a reciprocal love in conformity with the union and matrimonial surrender, in which each freely possesses the goods of both, which are the divine Essence, by reason of the voluntary delivery of one to the other; and they possess them both conjointly, saying to one another what the Son said to the Father in St. John (17:10): "All My goods are Thine; and Thy goods are Mine; and I am glorified in them."[35]

[35] *Obras y Vida de San Juan de la Cruz*, ed. R. P. Licinio, O.C.D., Madrid, 1955, Llama de Amer Viva, 3, 5, 78, p. 1234.

This is perfect love. Gerlac Peterssen, a friend of Thomas à Kempis, speaks of supernatural love in the same way:

> I see how greatly You love me, and that, if I remain in You, it is just as impossible that You should not love me at all times, in all places and in all ways, as that I should ever not love You. You give Yourself to me wholly, so that You are wholly and undividedly mine, as long as I am wholly and undividedly Yours. And if I am so wholly Yours, this means that You have loved me from the beginning of time. For this is nothing else than that You savor Yourself in me and that, through Your mercy, I savor You in myself and myself in You.[36]

Transformed by love, we speak that "new tongue," as our Lord promised the Apostles; we chant that "new canticle" on which the Psalmist, Pascal (Letter to Mlle. de Roannez), and Péguy (Commentary on Eve) dwell in admiration. We are endowed with a new sight; the delusive mirages, which we have seen as real, we now can see no more. Christ's lordship governs through love and guides our lives, as it governed the life of M. Olier:

> The Spirit of my Jesus vivifies me so that he seems to be my second soul, the soul of my soul. . . . All that He wills, I will. Whatever He commands, I do. What pleases Him, pleases me. What He does not want, I do not want. He is everything to me. He is in my hands to enable me to write, and to prevent me, when writing is not expedient.[37]

8. The Unity

Grace's supernatural love is all the worth of living, in time and in eternity. It is divine union with unity, in supernatural union of wills by which we totally will that love Substantial be all that He infinitely is, that He be ours, and that we be all His. This divine love needs love's handmaid, divine knowledge, and is accompanied by love's inseparable companion, divine happiness. This love is the only will that makes everything that it wills come true.

---

[36] *The Fiery Soliloquy with God*, London, 1921.
[37] *Esprit de M. Olier*, p. 153.

Blessed John Ruysbroeck, the "Admirable Doctor," guide of
Groote and à Kempis, expounded the mystical union of the soul
as contained in our Lord's words: "Behold, the spouse cometh; go
forth to meet him":

> Because they have abandoned themselves to God, in doing, in
> leaving undone, and in suffering, they have steadfast peace and
> inward joy, consolation and savor, in which the world cannot par-
> take, neither any dissembler, nor the man who seeks himself more
> than the glory of God. Moreover, those same inward and en-
> lightened men have before them in their inward seeing, whenever
> they will, the love of God, as something drawing and urging them
> in the Unity; for they see and feel that the Father and the Son,
> through the Holy Ghost, embrace each other and all the chosen,
> and draw themselves back with eternal love into the Unity of
> their Nature. Thus, the Unity is ever drawing to Itself and
> inviting to Itself everything that has been born of It, either by
> nature or by Grace. And therefore, too, such enlightened men are,
> with a free spirit, lifted up above reason into a bare and image-
> less vision, wherein lives the eternal indrawing summons of the
> divine Unity; and with an imageless and bare understanding, is
> drenched through by the eternal Brightness, even as the air is
> drenched through by sunshine. And the bare uplifted will is trans-
> formed and drenched through by abysmal Love, even as iron
> is by fire. And the bare uplifted memory feels itself enwrapped
> and established in an abysmal absence of image. And thereby,
> the created image is united, above reason in a threefold way, with
> its eternal Image, which is the origin of its being and its life. . . .
>   There all is full and overflowing; for the spirit feels itself to
> be one truth and one wealth and one unity with God. Yet even
> here there is an essential tending forward, and therein is an essen-
> tial distinction between the being of the soul and the Being
> of God. (Samuel c, 11.)[38]

St. John of the Cross, in the Augustinian tradition, proposes to us
the soul's reunion with God, by which we become like to the Holy
Trinity, fulfilling the assertion: "Beloved, now we are the children
of God . . . we shall be like him, for we shall see him just as he
is" (1 Jn. 3:2).

If one would learn how to find this Spouse, it must be recognized
that the Word, together with the Father and the Holy Spirit, is

[38] In *The Book of Supreme Truth,* transl. Dom Wynschenk, Dutton, N. Y., 1916.

hidden essentially in the inmost center of the soul [i.e., in the soul
as a spirit, operative in intelligence and free choice]. Therefore,
the soul, that would find Him through union of love, must go
forth and hide itself from all created things according to its own
will, and enter within itself in deepest recollection, communing
there with God in loving and affectionate fellowship, esteeming
all in this world as though it were not.[39]

Unitive love, blending our substance with the substance of God,
totally and irrevocably blends also our thinking and our loving with
the thinking and loving of God. Far more truly and intensely, what
Ovid sang of Aeneas as the object of Dido's love, can be said of
unitive love of God:

> Of Aeneas alone with wakeful eyes she thinks,
> Of Aeneas night and day she speaks to her soul.

On these lines of Ovid, Luis de Granada comments:

By this example, albeit human, those, who are not very spiritual,
can understand the condition and force of this divine love, which
we call unitive. It seizes and unites the soul with God, with so
great and incomprehensible suavity, that it does not allow us to
think or abide or rest in any other thing than in Him.[40]

We think often of those we love. The more we love a person, the
more the circumstances of our daily life raise associations with the
beloved in our mind. How much do I think of God? The answer to
this also answers the question: How much do I love God? Conversely,
too, the more we think of our ever present and most intimate Lord,
the more our unity with Him grows. Thought of God is sunlight
in which the fruit of love of God matures. Spiritual persons, like the
disciples on the road to Emmaus, thus "abide with Him all day" in
His association with our thought and activities. Of those who love
God but little, it is true that "in the midst of you there has stood
one whom you do not know" (Jn. 1:26).

So the great lover, Francis of Assisi, communed with God at the
sight of Brother Fire and Sister Water; and the constant song of
his troubadour heart was "Bless the Lord all His works!" The
beauties of nature are a vehicle carrying such a one to God, not a

---

[39] *Spiritual Canticle*, 1, 14.
[40] *Del Fin del Hombre*, 2, 24.

house in which to dwell in mere aesthetic pleasure. Francis was well aware that love is a fire that must be kept burning by ever feeding it with new fuel of acts of love. So taught St. Alphonsus Liguori:

> The fourth means to obtain perfect love is to train oneself to make acts of love frequently. A fire is fed by wood put on it; love is fed by acts of love.

To his novices he wrote:

> I urge you to be always making acts of love — at prayer, at Communion, during visits, during spiritual reading, in your cell, in the dining-room, while out walking, everywhere and at all times.[41]

The wise "Following of Christ" accentuates prayer for love and the practice of love:

> Enlarge me in love that I may learn to taste with the inward palate of my heart how sweet it is to love, to melt and bathe myself in love. . . . Let my soul quite lose itself in Thy praises, rejoicing exceedingly in love.[42]

We may well say *finis* to our meditation on love by recalling the Soliloquy of Hugh of St. Victor, in loving union with that Love which makes all things one:

> He is truly, my soul, thy Beloved Who visits thee. He comes invisible, He comes hidden, He comes incomprehensible. He comes to teach thee, not to be seen by thee. He comes to admonish thee that He may be understood by thee. He comes, not to pour His total Self into thee, but He affords Himself to be tasted; not to fulfill desire, but to draw attention. He offers some first fruits of His love. He does not offer the fullness of perfect satiety. And this is especially what belongs to the pledge of thy espousals, so that He will later give Himself to be seen and possessed perpetually. Now from time to time, in order that you may realize how pleasing He is, He offers Himself to be tasted. . . . I ask you my soul, . . . after all these gifts, acknowledge only One, love One, follow One, grasp One, possess One![43]

---

41 Give source.
42 Bk. 4, c. 5.
43 *De Arrha Animae, PL* 176, 970.

INDEX

Abandonment, to Christ, 162; and union, 179

Accidents, and hurt feelings, 54

Action, and the will, 180

Actions, human, 99

Activity, in and for God, 140

Act of love, how frequent, 103; virtual, 103

Acts, on Paul's conversion, 135

Adler, on the will to power, 65

Adoption, as child of God, 10

Agape, Eucharist as Love Feast, 36

Aloneness, total, without love of God, 119, 182

Alphonse Rodriguez, his lowly life of love, 181; and progress in perfection, 178

Alphonsus Liguori, on asking for love of God, 128; on bearing with faults, 68; on frequent acts of love, 188

Altruism, instinct toward, 19; and moral values, 16; obligation of, 18; as true egoism, 14

Americans, as lawless, 153

Angela di Foligno, on a mother's love, 157

Angelus Silesius, on becoming what you love, 132

Anger, cause of accidents, 54

Ansar (Arabian), and union in love, 183

Apostolate, of charity, 11

Approval, desire for, 70

Arbitration, place for, 92

Architecture, compensation in, 88

Aristotle, on the common good, 22; on friendship, man with God, 149

Art, compensation in, 88

Artists, love of beauty, 131

Astigmatism, spiritual, 23

Atheism, and brotherly love, 7

Atheists, as moralists, 19

Attachment, freedom from, 99

Augustine, St., on ascending to God through Christ, 171; on Christ as "loving Himself," 10; on Christ in our neighbor, 10, 44 f; on Christ's intercessary power, 142 f; on Christ's love of enemies, 56; on Christ's love as

our own, 116; on community of faults, 68; definition of love, 100; on divisions in human love, 180; on enemies of Christ, 55; on excuse for not loving God, 129; on the eye as example of charity, 28 f; on formal glory to God, 127; on fraternal love, the measure of love of God, 31; on God as charity, 11; on God's desire for love, 118; on God or self, 122 f; on growth of love, 121; on growth in virtue, 178; on harmony in monasteries, 32; on Holy Spirit as love, 139; on instinct to love God, 113, 114; on invitation to love, 139; on joy of baptism, 25; on love of enemies, 57; on love and free will, 105; on love as justifying, 106; on love and labor, 175; on love in Mystical Body, 93; on love that beautifies, 133; on loving all in God, 40, 108; on man's loves, 98; on need of love in life, 103; on penitent love, 136; on perfect love of God, 111; on return of love, 146; on seeing God in neighbor, 51; on self-love, 21; on total love of God, 111 f, 118; on transforming love, 164, 166; warning to detractors, 79

Basil, St., on God as love, 106

Beauty, and the artist, 131; beautifying, 131; Christ as, 132; and grace, 130; infinite in God, 129; licit love of, 131; natural, sign of God, 187; in order, 152; resulting from love, 60; source of, 7, 164

Bees, metamorphosis of, 171

Being, love of, 112

Belloc, H., on hatred of sin, 39

Benedict XV, on peace, 93

Benevolence, love of, 7

Bergson, Henri, on the love of mystics, 31 f

Bernard, St., on assimilation through love, 160; on return of love, 138; on solitude with God, 182

Billot, Cardinal, on ease of act of love, 103

189

Talebearing, effect of, 77; objective of, 71

Teachers, and secrets, 78

Tennyson, on likening effect of love, 164; on love and self, 174; on "new world which is the old," 173

Teresa of Avila, St., definition of Satan, 52; on God as our real good, 110; and increasing union with God, 177 f; influence of John of the Cross, 170; on two commandments, 29

Theology, as revealed law, 151

Thomas à Kempis, on possession of the one loved, 143; on sweetness of love, 188

Thomas Aquinas, St., on friendship, 149; on growth of love, 121; on law of love, 103; on love's aid to virtue, 151; on meaning of love, 100; on Mystical Body, 24; on reason for loving God, 15, 110; on transforming love, 161, 162; on unity of love, 6; on virtue and love, 6, 153

Thomas More, St., on bad use of time, 125

Thompson, Francis, on beauty in nature, 131; on bliss of solitude, 182; on God in all loves, 114; humble thought of, 150; on transforming love, 164

Thought, relation to love, 187; union of, 144; and writing, 180

Time, good use of, 125

Tobias and Raguel, 4

Tolerance, inexhaustible, 49; of opinions, 88

Totalitarianism, seed in Plato's Laws, 22

Transformation, into conformity with Christ, 171; by love, 160 f

Trinity, mirrored in man's love, 183; society of, 50

Truth, based on reason and faith, 49; and love, 50; priority of, 69; source of, 7

Turinaz, on universal law of love, 178

Understanding, true, 64

Union, marital, 166; personal, with God, 144; of souls, 179; of thought, 144; of wills, 143, 152, 160, 174, 185

United Nations, ideal, 90

Unity, effect of love, 102

Upanishads, on likening effect of love, 165

Value, moral, of altruistic action, 16

Vine, symbol of divine love, 166 f

Violence, in emergency, 91; essence of war, 93; irrational, 92; suppression of, 92

Virtue, based on charity, 6; dependent on love, 151

Vision, binocular, in love, 27

von Clausewitz, General, on war, 93

War, abnormal, 92; kinds of, 92; not inevitable, 90; unnecessary, 90

Welfare, dependent on love, 141

Will, action and, 180; habit of, 126

Will of God, acceptance of, 54; a "sacrament," 12

William of St. Thierry, on the Holy Spirit in us, 116

Wills, fusion of, 147; union of, 143, 152, 160, 174, 179, 185

Wilson, Fourteen Points, 90

Wisdom, on advice to rulers, 154; on the beauty of God, 130; on universality of love, 107

Word, The, substantial image of God, 163

Worship, and charity, 26

Worth, measure of, 8

Writing, relation to thought, 180

Wundt, on moral acts, 18